no appetite, while the conversation in general consisted of flying phrases referring to the great impending event of the great day, that had already dawned.

"Seem to has St Julians, Fitz?" s.d a youth of very tender years, & whose countenance fair visage was as downy & as blooming as the peach ... with a languid air, he withdrew his lips to make this enquiry of one of the conspicuous the gentlemen with the cave —

"Yes; why were not you there?"

CHRISTOPHER HIBBERT

DISRAELI
and his world

with 111 illustrations

THAMES AND HUDSON

FOR LUCY

Half-title: Manuscript page, in
Disraeli's own hand, from *Sybil*,
published in 1845. The novel
presented a society divided into
'Two Nations' – the Rich and the
Poor

Frontispiece: Disraeli as a young man,
a portrait by Sir Francis Grant

Picture research: Alla Weaver

Printed in Great Britain by Jarrold and Sons Ltd, Norwich

RECALLING HIS FIRST DAYS AT BOARDING-SCHOOL in the early years of the nineteenth century, an elderly Victorian clergyman remembered most vividly a boy named Ben into whose care he had been entrusted. 'I looked up to him as a big boy,' the clergyman said, 'and very kind he was to me, making me sit next to him in play hours, and amusing me with stories of robbers and caves, illustrating them with rough pencil sketches which he continually rubbed out to make way for fresh ones. He was a very rapid reader, was fond of romances, and would often let me sit by him and read the same book, good-naturedly waiting before turning a leaf till he knew I had reached the bottom of the page.'

Other former pupils at the school remembered Ben as a lively, cheerful, carefree boy who took scant trouble over his lessons, who amused his companions on wet half holidays by reciting romantic adventures of his own composition, and who 'had a taste not uncommon among schoolboys for little acts of bargaining and merchandise'. Being a Jew he was allowed to stand at the back of the classroom during prayers and to receive instruction in Hebrew from a rabbi on Saturdays. At the end of term he 'went home for the holidays in the basket of the Blackheath coach, [firing] away at the passers-by with his pea-shooter'.

His home at that time was a comfortable house overlooking Gray's Inn where he had been born on 21 December 1804. His father was

Benjamin Disraeli's birthplace, 6 King's Road, Bedford Row (later renamed 22 Theobald's Road), overlooked Gray's Inn Gardens (*above*). *Below:* Disraeli as a child. The miniaturist Cosway was a friend of his parents

CURIOSITIES OF LITERATURE,

BY

I. D'ISRAELI, ESQ.
D.C.L. F.S.A.

A New Edition.

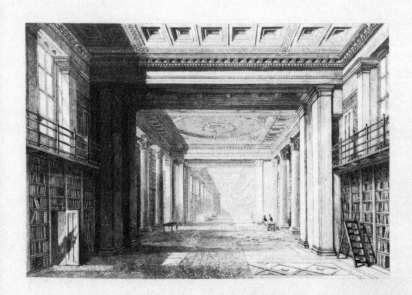

Isaac D'Israeli, a respected man of letters of independent means and Italian descent, the first two volumes of whose best-known work, *Curiosities of Literature*, had been published some years before. His mother was Maria Basevi, a lady from an ancient Jewish family, one of whose illustrious forebears was a leader of the great exodus of his race from Spain in 1492. Her son, Ben, was extremely proud of his Jewish ancestry, considering himself of highly aristocratic birth, exaggerating in a characteristically romantic way the family's past glories and, unaware of his mother's distinguished descent, making unwarranted claims for that of his father.

Everyone liked his father, a kindly unassuming though rather fussy man who spent most of his time at home, compiling anthologies, writing all kinds of books, emerging from his library, a small black velvet cap over his long curly hair, to talk loquaciously and disjointedly over his meals. When he went out it was usually to visit the British Museum, to browse in a bookshop, or to see his publisher, John Murray. 'He was a complete literary character,' his son wrote of him affectionately in later years. 'Even marriage [contracted at the age of thirty-five] produced no change: he rose to enter the chamber where he lived alone with his books, and at night his lamp was ever lit within the same walls. . . . He disliked business, and he never required relaxation. . . . If he entered a club, it was only to go into the library. In the country, he scarcely ever left his room but to saunter in abstraction upon a terrace; muse over a chapter, or coin a sentence.'

Benjamin's parents. His father's father had come from Cento, near Ferrara, in the mid-eighteenth century; his mother, a quiet and modest figure, married Isaac when he was thirty-five

Opposite: From the days when he shocked his parents by condemning commerce as 'the Corruption of Mankind', Isaac D'Israeli's life revolved around literature. As this title-page of 1838 indicates, his best-known book, *Curiosities of Literature*, remained in print long after its first publication

BAPTISMS solemnized in the Parish of *St. Andrew Holborn London*
in the County of *Middlesex* in the Year 18 17

When Baptized.	Child's Christian Name.	Parents Name.		Abode.	Quality, Trade, or Profession.	By whom the Ceremony was performed.
		Christian.	Surname.			
1817. July 31 No. 633.	Benjamin Son of Said to be	Isaac & Maria about 12	D'Israeli	Kings Road	gentleman	J. ꞓ

He was not the least interested in politics, which he claimed not to understand, nor in the affairs of the synagogue to which he paid his dues only out of deference to his father, a devout conformist member of the Sephardi congregation at Bevis Marks. When his father died, and he felt released from this filial obligation, he asked the Elders to remove his own name from the list of synagogue members; and, although he never became a Christian himself, he was persuaded by a Christian friend to allow Benjamin to be baptized, as well as his daughter, Sarah, and Benjamin's two younger brothers, Raphael and Jacobus, thereafter known as Ralph and James.

Having already inherited a fortune from his grandmother (who cut her daughter out of her will for expressing contempt for the Jewish faith), Isaac D'Israeli, by the additional accession of his father's money, was now enabled to move into a larger and even more comfortable house, 6 Bloomsbury Square, which had for him the fine advantage of being just round the corner from the British Museum. Soon after this move, Benjamin was sent to a new school. Winchester, where his two younger brothers were to go, was considered but rejected in favour of Higham Hall in Epping Forest, a small academy kept by a Unitarian

Bloomsbury Square in the late eighteenth century; the Disraeli home at No. 6 was ideally located for Isaac to pursue his reading in the British Museum

Opposite: Benjamin Disraeli was baptized at St Andrew's Church, Holborn. *Above:* the church, which was built in 1686 from designs by Wren, as it was in the year of Disraeli's birth. *Below:* the entry in the baptismal register, 31 July 1817

Disraeli's grandmother, Sarah, had brought a useful dowry to her husband. When Benjamin visited her as a schoolboy, she seems to have shown herself an unsympathetic, unfriendly figure

minister, a most learned scholar of whom Isaac D'Israeli had formed a high opinion after having met him in a bookshop. The school was run on the lines of a public school: Latin and Greek were taught to the exclusion of almost every other subject. But Benjamin did not have to attend chapel every day as he would have had to do at Winchester. Instead, he had to walk to the nearest church on Sundays with the other Anglican boys, while the rest of the school attended a Unitarian service. This was considered no hardship until it was discovered that by the time the Church of England pupils returned to school the Sunday dinner was almost finished, a deprivation which prompted Benjamin to propose that he and his Anglican companions should become Unitarians during term time.

Benjamin remained at Higham Hall for only a few terms. By the beginning of 1820 he was studying at home in his father's library, improving his knowledge of Latin, though not progressing very far in Greek, reading a great deal of history and English literature, listing the works he read and his precociously confident opinions of them in a diary which reveals a desire to acquire wide knowledge rather than deep understanding. He had already made up his mind, so he afterwards declared, that he would one day make his way into the House of Commons; and his brother Ralph related how fond he was of 'playing at Parliament', always reserving for himself the part of Prime Minister or at least of a senior Cabinet member, relegating the others to the benches of the Opposition.

His father – though normally inclined to indulge rather than to coerce his children – had other ideas, however, about his eldest son's career. He pressed him to become a lawyer, answering the boy's protests by drawing his attention to the example of Philip Carteret Webb, a distinguished Member of Parliament who had begun his career in a solicitor's office. So, in November 1821, when he was nearly seventeen, Benjamin Disraeli (as, dropping the apostrophe, he chose to spell his name) became an articled clerk in one of the City's leading firms of solicitors. 'My business was to be the private secretary of the busiest partner,' he recorded, maintaining that, while he often regretted not having gone to university, the time he spent with the firm was far from wasted. 'He dictated to me every day his correspondence, which was as extensive as a Minister's, and when the clients arrived I did not leave the room, but remained not only to learn my business but to become acquainted with my future clients. They were in general men of great importance – bank directors, East India directors, merchants. . . . It gave me great facility with my pen and no inconsiderable knowledge of human nature.'

But like Charles Dickens, who was to start work as a clerk in a smaller firm of solicitors a few years later, Disraeli did not take to the law. He performed his duties adequately, yet he yearned for other things. He became pensive and restless. The books he read in his father's library, the distinguished men he met at work, and the conversation he heard at John Murray's dinner-table, to which he was now occasionally invited with his father, stirred his imagination and ambition. He seemed to himself worthy of a more dramatic future than that promised by the testaments and conveyances, the registers and ledgers of Frederick's Place, Old Jewry. Setting himself apart from the other clerks, he adopted a style of dress which was considered striking even in those early years of the reign of George IV when the clothes and affectations of the dandies were providing such outlandish copy for the pen of George Cruikshank. The wife of one of the partners in the firm described him as calling at her house in a black velvet suit with ruffles and black stockings with red clocks. His appearance and manner were entirely fitted, so she said, to this 'rather conspicuous attire'. Dark and handsome with thick, curly black hair, rings upon the fingers of both well-shaped hands, he would stand in his frilled shirt and tight pantaloons, with legs crossed and elbow on fireplace, flamboyant and theatrical, delivering himself of high-flown compliments and sharp asides as though to the manner born. 'You have too much genius for Frederick's Place,' another lady said to him one day, much to his satisfaction. 'It will never do!'

It was not to do. There was some inconclusive talk of his going to Oxford; but it was eventually an illness which provided an excuse for

The young Disraeli. Justin McCarthy, who wrote a history spanning Disraeli's career, described him in these early days as 'an eccentric and audacious adventurer, who was kept from being dangerous by the affectations and absurdities of his conduct'

his escaping from Frederick's Place and for his going on a tour of the Continent. In company with his father, who had also been ill, and William George Meredith, one of Benjamin's most intimate friends, he sailed for Ostend in July 1824. In lively, detailed letters to his sister, to whom he was devoted, Disraeli described the journey through Bruges, Antwerp and Brussels to Cologne, Mainz and Heidelberg, commenting on the places and works of art he saw, informing her that the road to Spa was 'a perfect debauch of gorgeous scenery'; that Ems was a 'very Castle of Indolence' where residents and visitors alike, 'lounging and lackadaisical, bask on sunny banks or doze in acacia arbors'; assuring her that the Governor, who always booked rooms at the 'crack hotels', was 'particularly well'; and that he himself had become 'a most exquisite billiard player'. He dwelt upon the fine wines which they 'unsealed and floored with equal rapidity'; and, in even more loving detail, upon the food they ate, reciting long menus of fricandeaux and joints and chops, capital roast pigeons and wonderfully fine dishes of peas, salads of delicate crispness and silvery whiteness, 'frogs, *pâté de grenouilles* – magnificent! sublime!' Descending the 'magical waters' of the Rhine he came to his final determination 'not to be a lawyer'.

Cologne, where (Disraeli wrote home to his sister) 'We were almost stopped in our progress by the stares of the multitude, who imagined we were Archdukes at least'

Overleaf: The romantic Rhine. 'I determined when descending those magical waters that I would not be a lawyer'

Disraeli's office at 6 Frederick's Place, Old Jewry. 'The Bar: pooh! . . . to succeed as an advocate, I must be a great lawyer, and to be a great lawyer, I must give up my chance of being a great man'

Certainly, on his return to England, he did not go back to Frederick's Place. Presumably under pressure from his father, however, he agreed to read for the Bar and was admitted as a student of Lincoln's Inn in November 1824. But by then he had made up his mind not to wait a moment longer for any fame or fortune that the law might ultimately bring him. Already he had tried his hand at writing, and had managed to complete a novel which he sent to Murray except for two chapters which he said he had lost. Murray kept the rest of the novel so long that the author was driven to conclude that he did not think it worth publishing. And, to save himself the humiliation of positive rejection, he wrote to Murray – making sly allusion to the recent destruction of Byron's memoirs – to say, 'As you have had some small experience in burning manuscripts perhaps you will be so kind as to consign [my novel] to the flames.'

Having failed to make his mark as a novelist, Disraeli, with a career in Parliament still in view, now set his mind to making money. So, in association with an articled clerk, whom he had met while working at Frederick's Place, and with the son of a wealthy stockbroker, he began to speculate in mining shares, at the same time writing pamphlets which made dubious and sometimes reckless claims on behalf of

various South American and Mexican mining companies in which he and his associates – as well as John Murray, the pamphlets' publisher – had invested their money. Disraeli, of course, had little money to invest; and when the market collapsed, he not only lost it all, but found himself so heavily in debt that it was years before he could extricate himself.

Apparently undeterred by this catastrophe, which revealed him as both ingenuous and none too scrupulous in matters of finance, Disraeli plunged enthusiastically into another venture with Murray and a leading South American merchant, J. D. Powles. This was to found a daily newspaper, an ambition long cherished by Murray whose *Quarterly Review* was one of the most successful periodicals of the time. Disraeli, fanning Murray's ambition by his youthful energy and high spirits, hurried about London talking to lawyers and printers, engaging correspondents, interviewing reporters and sub-editors and discussing with his cousin, the architect George Basevi, plans for the paper's new offices in Great George Street. Twice he went to Scotland to see J. G. Lockhart, Sir Walter Scott's son-in-law, who was evidently to be enlisted as a leading contributor. Yet this excited activity was all in vain. The newspaper, for which Disraeli chose the

J. G. Lockhart, who was energetically courted by Disraeli in developing his plans for the *Representative*

Sarah and Benjamin Austen. Sarah was responsible for securing publication of Disraeli's first book, *Vivian Grey*, and then – with her husband – for taking abroad the downcast author, who had been shocked by the criticism of the pretensions his book revealed

name, the *Representative*, made its long-delayed appearance in January 1825. But by then Powles had been ruined, and, since Disraeli had no money anyway, Murray was left alone to bear its expenses. These were as heavy as the contents of the paper were tedious, ill-edited and clumsily displayed. After a few months the *Representative* expired, unlamented even by those few readers who had troubled to peruse its stodgy pages. Murray lost over £25,000.

In later years Disraeli did not care to discuss this early failure in his career; but at the time his disappointment did not last long, and, resilient as ever, he was soon hard at work on another novel. The year before, Robert Ward, from whom Isaac D'Israeli had rented a country-house, had anonymously published *Tremaine or the Man of Refinement*, 'a novel of fashionable life', which had enjoyed a considerable success. In conscious imitation of this style of novel, Disraeli now produced *Vivian Grey*, the story of a clever, unscrupulous, ambitious and charming young man who attempts to succeed in life by his wits and reckless temerity but who is left at the end 'knowing himself to be the most unfortunate and unhappy man that ever existed'.

Having finished this ill-constructed but vibrant and entertaining book in a matter of months, Disraeli sent the manuscript to Sarah

Austen, 'a woman of more than ordinary talent', in the words of her nephew, 'and of more than ordinary beauty, very jealous of shining in society and fond of flattery and admiration'. She was the childless wife of Benjamin Austen, Robert Ward's solicitor and agent who was a friend of the D'Israeli family; and Disraeli, a master of flattery, particularly of women older than himself, had soon persuaded Mrs Austen that he was a young man whom she would very much like to help. She expressed herself 'quite delighted' with the manuscript, and not only offered to recommend it to Henry Colburn, Ward's publisher, but also to copy it out in her own hand, so that the secret of its authorship should be preserved – it being naturally understood that books of this nature sold much better if the author could be supposed to be a fashionable gentleman rather than a professional novelist. Colburn, who readily accepted the novel for publication when Sarah Austen pressed it upon him, did his utmost to ensure the public that *Vivian Grey* was, indeed, by a gentleman well qualified to reveal the foibles and eccentricities of the *beau monde*. 'By the by,' Colburn remarked one day to the editor of a magazine in which he hoped the novel would be reviewed; 'I have a capital book out – *Vivian Grey*. The authorship is a great secret – a man of high fashion – very high – keeps the first society. I can assure you it is a most piquant and spirited work, quite sparkling.'

John Murray's drawing-room at 50 Albemarle Street. Isaac D'Israeli is seated far left and John Murray II himself is immediately to his right; Sir Walter Scott and Byron stand together far right. Benjamin Disraeli was to be influenced considerably by his father's literary circle of friends, though he never met Byron

On its first appearance the book was well received. One critic remarked that 'the class of the author was a little betrayed by his frequent references to topics of which the mere man of fashion knows nothing and cares less'. But most readers, as Robert Ward told Sarah Austen, praised its 'wit, raciness and boldness'. They discussed the models for the various characters and wondered about the identity of their creator. Once the secret was discovered, however, and it became known that the author was a middle-class Jew no more than twenty-one years old, the reviewers rose up vituperatively to condemn him for his 'most ludicrous affectation of good breeding', the absurd solecisms in 'a paltry catchpenny' the dubious merits of which had been preposterously inflated by 'shameful and shameless puffery'.

Disraeli was deeply wounded by all this 'malignant and adroit ridicule', and in later editions of the book took the most elaborate care to correct the impression that he had not always been familiar with the fashionable world. But he could not undo the damage he had done by recklessly caricaturing John Murray as the Marquess of Carabas. He endeavoured to rectify his mistake by rewriting the passages detailing the Marquess's bibulous loquacity. Yet Murray could not forgive him for his 'outrageous breach of all confidence'; and although he later published two of Disraeli's other books, he made it clear that he did so purely as a publisher: their friendship was broken, never to be resumed.

Nor was Murray the only enemy whom Disraeli heedlessly made at this time. For just before the publication of *Vivian Grey* there appeared the first number of a satirical weekly journal, the *Star Chamber*. Disraeli was subsequently driven to deny that he was this magazine's editor; but it was widely believed that he was far more closely concerned with its contents than was its nominal editor, a friend of William George Meredith, who was also its proprietor. Disraeli was one of its principal contributors; and, even if he did not write the satirical attacks on Murray and his friends which appeared in its pages, they could not fail to resent the young Disraeli's connection with so scurrilous a publication. Both Lockhart and John Wilson Croker, a friend of the future Prime Minister, Sir Robert Peel, as well as Murray, had cause to be offended by the *Star Chamber*; and all these men had widespread influence in the world into which Disraeli hoped one day to break. He had certainly not made a promising start for a man intent upon a public career of fame and fortune. Those who knew him well found him kind, affectionate and generous; but he was also vain, reckless, impulsive and unpredictable, taking an excessive pleasure in mysterious and conspiratorial dealings and in his picture of himself as a romantic adventurer parading glittering talents before an astonished world.

Opposite: Disraeli in his mid-twenties, 1828. 'Beware of endeavouring to become a great man in a hurry', his father warned

Visiting the Brera in Milan, Disraeli showed special interest in Guercino's *Abraham dismissing Hagar.* He was, it seems, unaware that his grandfather's home town had been Cento, birthplace of Guercino; the D'Israeli family had themselves possessed two paintings by that artist

Run down in health and thankful for an opportunity to escape from England, Disraeli now eagerly accepted an invitation from the Austens to go on holiday with them through Switzerland to northern Italy. They sailed from Dover, posted through Dijon to Geneva, and arrived in Milan at the beginning of September 1826. On the way Disraeli, as he excitedly told his father, met Maurice, Lord Byron's celebrated boatman, a 'very handsome man and very vain' who talked of nothing but the poet. Disraeli persuaded Maurice to row him on the lake 'at all hours', and to regale him with stories about the extraordinary, 'ludicrously ostentatious *milor*', his prowess as a swimmer, his breakfasts of 'three or four bottles of the richest wines'. Disraeli's letters home were gay and entertaining; and the Austens confirmed that he was vastly improved in health and looks, enjoying everything. 'Your brother is so easily pleased, so accommodating, so amusing, and so actively kind,' Sarah Disraeli was told by Mrs Austen, who seems to have fallen rather in love with him. 'I shall always reflect upon . . . our journey with the greatest pleasure.'

Disraeli's sister Sarah. The two were very close

After two months' absence, Disraeli returned to England in excellent spirits, having spent scarcely more than £150, including £20 for prints and presents, and bringing back with him several chapters of a sequel to *Vivian Grey*. Although it was nothing like so entertaining as the first book, Colburn offered him an advance of £500, well over twice as much as he had had before. Soon after receiving it, however, Disraeli's high spirits suddenly collapsed; and, as in the case of a manic depressive, from excited gaiety he sank into a trough of gloomy despair. His doctor, baffled by the true nature of his nervous breakdown, described it as 'a chronic inflammation of the membranes of the brain'. He remained ill for many months. 'My son's life,' his father commented in January 1829, 'within the last year and a half, with a very slight exception, has been a blank in his existence.' During this time he managed to produce another novel, a flat, weak satire on the Utilitarians which Colburn published as *The Voyage of Captain Popanilla*. But recurrent headaches and black depression prevented him from attempting any other work, as he followed his

The D'Israeli country home,
Bradenham Manor,
Buckinghamshire

family from one rented country-house to the next, worried by his debts
and, as he confessed to Lady Derby in his old age, devoured by
ambition which he saw no means of gratifying. 'Whether I shall ever
do anything which may mark me out from the crowd I know not,' he
wrote to a friend. 'I am one of those to whom moderate reputation can
give no pleasure, and who in all probability, am incapable of achieving
a great one.'

At length he came to the conclusion that another, more prolonged
absence from England was the only hope for him. And, as his father
'fairly knocked on the head' this idea of a tour of the Mediterranean
and the Far East and, though usually 'too indulgent', refused to pay for
it, he was compelled, as he told Benjamin Austen, to 'hack for it'. The
result of this determination was *The Young Duke*, a readable, if rather
absurd novel of fashionable life in the manner of *Vivian Grey*. Colburn,
sure of the market for such works, again offered £500 and this, together
with a loan from Austen, enabled Disraeli to complete his plans for his
Grand Tour. He asked William George Meredith, who was now
engaged to his sister, Sarah, to go with him; and the two men planned
to set out at the end of May 1830.

Cheered by this prospect and by the imminent appearance of *The
Young Duke* which he felt confident would be a great success and
'complete the corruption of the public taste', Disraeli flung off his
illness and became as animated as he had formerly been morose. He
came up to London from the house at Bradenham, near High

Wycombe where his father had now finally settled, wearing 'a blue surtout, a pair of military light blue trousers and black stockings with red stripes'. 'The people quite made way for me as I passed,' he told Meredith. 'It was like the opening of the Red Sea.'

'I should think so!' Meredith commented, amazed by his attire. 'He was in excellent spirits, full of schemes for the projected journey to Stamboul and Jerusalem; full, as usual, also of capital stories, but he could make a story out of nothing.' For dinner with the novelist, Edward Lytton Bulwer, he changed into 'green velvet trousers, a canary coloured waistcoat, low shoes, silver buckles, lace at his wrists, and his hair in ringlets'. His conversation, so Bulwer's brother Henry recalled, was as vivid as his clothes.

Disraeli's health continued to improve throughout the sixteen months of his tour, which was to have so profound an effect on his future political and literary career. He revelled in the sunshine which always made his spirits glow; he delighted in the places he visited and the people he met; his long, amusing, vivid letters to his family bear

Maria D'Israeli in 1828. Benjamin does not seem to have found emotional comfort in a close relationship with his mother

'I lived for a week among brigands and wandered in the fantastic halls of the delicate Alhambra'

eloquent testimony to the intense pleasure he derived from every splendid scene and strange encounter. At Gibraltar he decided that Lady Don, the Governor's wife, was the most charming woman he had ever met. In Spain – where he 'travelled through the whole of Andalusia on horseback', cheered at bull-fights, was enchanted by Murillo and found Cadiz more beautiful than Florence – he ate everything that was put before him and was delighted when the woman who showed him over the Alhambra refused to believe he was not a Moor. On Malta he discovered the pleasures of tobacco and took to 'sitting in an easy chair, with a Turkish pipe six feet long'. In Albania he became 'quite a Turk', squatted on a divan, made up such

a costume from his 'heterogeneous wardrobe' that the Grand Vizier's entourage, who were 'mad on the subject of dress, were utterly astounded', and derived a thrill of delight from being made much of by a man who was 'daily decapitating half the province'. In Athens, which he found all that he could have wished, he prided himself on being the first Englishman to whom the Acropolis had been opened since the war of liberation from the Turks. In Constantinople he thought the lazy, sensual life of ottomans and scented baths far 'more sensible than all the bustle of clubs, all the boring of drawing-rooms, and all the coarse vulgarity of our political controversies'. He was 'thunderstruck' by Jerusalem where he spent 'the most delightful'

The rhythms and atmosphere of Eastern life had considerable appeal for the young Disraeli

Overleaf: In Jerusalem he was overwhelmed by the Mosque of Omar, traditional site of the temple of his distant ancestors. 'I caught a glorious glimpse of splendid courts, and light airy gates of Saracenic triumph, flights of noble steps, long arcades, and interior gardens . . .'

Mosque of Omar Shewing the Site of the Temple.

week in all his travels. He was entranced, too, by Egypt where he remained for several months and where he met Mehemet Ali, who discussed with him the idea of introducing parliamentary democracy into the country. 'I will have as many Parliaments as the King of England himself,' the Pasha is alleged to have said to him. 'But I have made up my mind, to prevent inconvenience, to elect them myself.'

On Malta, Disraeli and Meredith came across James Clay, a rich, witty young man, a future Member of Parliament with an insatiable appetite for women. And, evidently encouraged by Clay, in whose chartered yacht they were to sail from Malta to Corfu, Disraeli became even more outlandish in dress and affected in manner than he had been in Gibraltar where he had, so he claimed, not only maintained his reputation of being 'a great judge of costume, to the admiration and envy of many subalterns', but had also enjoyed 'the fame of being the first who ever passed the Straits with two canes, a morning and an evening cane'. On Malta he paraded about Valetta in a 'majo jacket, white trousers, and a sash of all the colours in the rainbow', followed by 'one-half the population of the place and putting a stop to all business'. He was very popular with the British officers, so he assured his father. For, 'affectation tells here even better than wit. Yesterday, at the racket court, sitting in the gallery among strangers, the ball entered and lightly struck me and fell at my feet. I picked it up, and observing a young rifleman excessively stiff, I humbly requested him to forward its passage into the court, as I had really never thrown a ball in my life. This incident has been the general subject of conversation at all the messes to-day!'

In fact, Disraeli's affectations do not appear to have been so admired as he supposed. Clay was later quoted as having said that while Disraeli was a most agreeable and natural companion 'when they were by themselves, when they got into society, his coxcombry was intolerable. . . . He made himself so hateful to the officers' mess that . . . they ceased to invite "that damned bumptious Jew boy".'

Whether or not he realized how offensive some of his less volatile countrymen found him, Disraeli remained as exhibitionistic as ever. In Cairo, however, his flamboyance was subdued by a tragedy which affected him deeply. On 19 July 1831 Meredith died of smallpox.

'It is too terrible to believe,' Disraeli wrote home in an emotional letter to his father. 'I would willingly have given my life for his. . . . Oh! my father, why do we live? The anguish of my soul is great. Our innocent lamb, our angel is stricken. Save her, save her. I will come home directly. . . . I wish to live only for my sister. I think of her day and night.' To his 'own Sa' he wrote, 'Oh! my sister, in this hour of overwhelming affliction my thoughts are only for you. . . . My beloved, be my genius, my solace, my companion, my joy. We will never part,

Egypt offered the pyramids and the
chance to meet Mehemet Ali, who
suggested that no pure Englishman
could have the ability to walk so
softly as Disraeli

Tita, adventurer and gondolier to
Lord Byron. After Byron's death he
had fought for the Greeks; Disraeli
rescued him from destitution in
Malta and brought him back to
England

and if I cannot be to you all our lost friend was, at least we will feel that
life can never be a blank while gilded by the perfect love of a sister and a
brother.'

Sarah, overwhelmed by grief, took solace from this letter. She was
twenty-eight now, and she never considered marriage again. For the
rest of her life she devoted herself to the welfare of her parents and her
brothers, particularly to Benjamin whom she admired as much as she
adored. For the next few years she was his most intimate confidante.
'He rarely spoke of his sister . . . but that was his habit where his feelings
were deeply concerned,' commented his close friend, Sir Philip Rose.
'On the first occasion of his becoming Prime Minister I remember
saying to him, "If only your sister had been alive now to witness your
triumph what happiness it would have given her"; and he replied,
"Ah, poor Sa, poor Sa! We've lost our audience. We've lost our
audience."'

Despite the death of his friend and the pity he felt for his sister,
Disraeli's mood on arriving home was one of cheerful optimism – 'in

famous condition,' as he put it himself, 'full of hope and courage'. He had been working on two novels while he was abroad, *Contarini Fleming* and *The Wondrous Tale of Alroy*, and he entertained high hopes for both of them, particularly for the first. Indeed, he confided to his diary that he considered *Contarini Fleming* 'the perfection of English prose and a chef d'œuvre'. The public did not agree with him. The novel, little read today except for what it reveals of the author's own early life and temperament, was a financial disaster. And while *Alroy*, which was written in a kind of poetic prose, often bathetic and sometimes ludicrous, was more remunerative, enabling him to pay off a few of his still burdensome debts, most critics were not impressed. 'O reader dear!' one of them wrote in amusing parody. 'Do pray look here, and you will spy the curly hair and forehead fair, and nose so high and gleaming eye of Benjami Disraeli, the wondrous boy who wrote *Alroy*, in rhyme and prose, only to show how long ago victorious Judah's lion-banner rose.'

Disraeli was not dismayed. He had returned home in perfect health, and a venereal disease which he appears to have contracted in a brothel in St James's Street was cleared up by a six weeks' course of mercury. Taking lodgings in Duke Street, he eagerly accepted the invitations which were offered him. His provenance was not such as to gain him entry into the greatest houses, but less particular hostesses, encouraged by Edward Lytton Bulwer, welcomed his company and enjoyed his sprightly, fertile, witty conversation. He was entertained by Lady Cork, Lady Dudley Stuart and Lady Charleville; he became a regular guest at Lady Blessington's house in Seamore Place and a close friend

Edward Lytton Bulwer, brilliant dandy, whose first book *Pelham* was far better received than Disraeli's *Vivian Grey*. He also beat Disraeli to a seat in Parliament

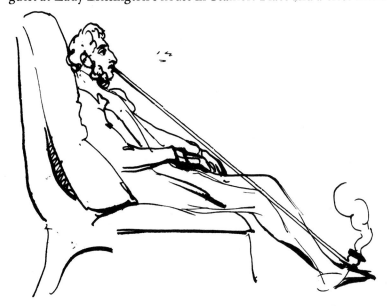

Lady Blessington, according to Edward Lytton Bulwer, had 'a singularly sweet and gracious face, and a wonderful symmetry of form' – until she grew too fat

of Lady Blessington's lover, the attractive, egotistical, inordinately extravagant Count D'Orsay, the husband of her stepdaughter and the acknowledged arbiter of dandiacal fashion. At Lady Blessington's Disraeli was introduced to Lord Durham; at the Opera he met William Beckford; at Lord Eliot's he sat next to Sir Robert Peel who – so he confidently assured his sister in letters which boast outrageously of his social success – was 'in a most condescending mood' and, having 'attacked his turbot almost exclusively with his knife', 'unbent with becoming haughtiness'.

In fact, Peel's impressions of the apparently over-confident but perhaps rather nervous young man were not so favourable as Disraeli believed or liked to pretend. 'From his appearance or manner Sir Robert Peel seemed to take an intuitive dislike to him,' wrote a friend of Eliot's who was also of the party, and, after Disraeli had asked Peel to lend him some papers for a book he was writing, Peel '"buried his chin in his neckcloth," to use [Eliot's] own expression; and did not speak a word to Disraeli during the rest of the meal'.

Alfred d'Orsay

Count D'Orsay, whose arranged
marriage to Lady Blessington's
schoolgirl daughter Harriet was the
subject of much society gossip

Sir Robert Peel (*left*) was fluent but
without the least style, said Disraeli
(*right*, drawn in 1834 by Count
D'Orsay). Peel 'buried his chin in
his neckcloth' and ignored Disraeli
during much of dinner at their first
meeting

Peel was far from being the only person whom Disraeli offended.
Disraeli himself continued to assure his sister that he was the greatest
social success both in London and in the country where he 'hunted the
other day with Sir Henry Smythe's hounds and although not in scarlet
was the best mounted man in the field . . . and stopped at nothing'. He
related a conversation between Lord Carrington and Lady Cork who
was alleged to have said to 'the old Lord', 'Why [Disraeli] is the best
ton in London! There is not a party that goes down without him. The
Duchess of Hamilton says there is nothing like him. Lady Lonsdale
would give her head and shoulders for him.' Certainly, there were
those who were overwhelmed by his brilliance. An American who
met him at Lady Blessington's thought him the 'most wonderful
talker' he had ever had the fortune to meet. 'He is satirical,
contemptuous, pathetic, humorous, everything in a moment. Add to
this that Disraeli's face is the most intellectual face in England – pale,
regular, and overshadowed with the most luxuriant masses of raven-
black hair.'

Yet there were many others who were exasperated by him; by his
habit of pontificating with his thumbs tucked into the armholes of his
waistcoat; by his irritating practice of prefacing his remarks with an
incantation, picked up in the Near East, 'Allah is great!'; by his

elaborate affectations of weary boredom on being asked to meet someone whom he did not wish to know. It caused little surprise when his candidature for membership of the Athenaeum was blackballed, even though his father had helped to found the club. An attempt to join Crockford's was similarly unsuccessful.

Nor did he at first succeed when he tried to get into Parliament. His ambitions as a politician had been publicly announced at a party given by the Hon. Caroline Norton where he met Lord Melbourne. 'Well now, tell me, what do you want to be?' Melbourne asked him after they had been talking together for some time. 'I want', the young man replied, 'to be Prime Minister.' Melbourne 'gave a long sigh'.

The Hon. Caroline Norton, with her grandfather Sheridan in the background. Her relationship with Lord Melbourne eventually prompted her husband to allege adultery in the law-courts

Disraeli had not yet decided, though, to which party to commit himself. He had an instinctive dislike of the Whigs, but had not yet otherwise developed any strong political inclinations. In any case, he felt drawn to Westminster not, it seems, by any sense of public service but by ambition and vanity, the desire for fame, the need, perhaps, to compensate for an inner insecurity by making himself remarkable. Realizing that it might prove fatal to attach himself to a falling star, he shied away from the Tories whose influence was rapidly waning, and made up his mind to present himself as a Radical.

'Toryism is worn out,' he told Benjamin Austen as he left to stand as a candidate in the by-election at High Wycombe in June 1832, 'and I cannot condescend to be a Whig. . . . I start in the high Radical interest.' He started in grand style, making an impassioned speech from the portico of the Red Lion which astonished his audience who had expected something far less robust from this dandified Jew with his cambric cuffs and flowing curls. But although the Reform Bill had just become law, voting in this election was still confined to the few names on the old register; and most of those who might have voted for the young Radical were not entitled to do so. No more than thirty-two votes were cast; and Disraeli received only twelve of them.

He was undismayed, however. In December that year Parliament was dissolved and a general election was held on the new register. The electorate at High Wycombe was increased to nearly three hundred; and he was convinced that this time he would succeed. So confident of success was he, indeed, that he ordered a chair to be made in his electioneering colours of pink and white so that he could be carried in triumph through the streets of the town by his jubilant supporters. But the electorate of High Wycombe did not choose to have it so. He received scarcely more than a third of the number of votes cast for his opponents.

His determination to get into the House of Commons strengthened rather than dissipated by these setbacks, Disraeli now looked to other constituencies, issuing addresses which display a willingness to trim his views to suit the different electorates. These efforts, though, were in vain. And, after a third defeat at High Wycombe as an independent Radical in 1834, Disraeli came to the conclusion that if he were to succeed he must join one of the two main parties. So, having decided that he would still have nothing to do with the Whigs, and encouraged by Lord Lyndhurst, the former Tory Lord Chancellor, who, despite the difference in their ages had become an intimate friend, Disraeli made up his mind to throw in his lot with the Conservatives after all. He had his name put down for the Carlton Club; and, after some pressure had been applied to the election committee by his proposers and by friends of Lady Blessington, he was appointed.

Thereafter he was regularly seen at the dinner-tables of leading Conservatives, the affectation of his conversation much abated. And in April 1835 he was invited to become the official Tory candidate at Taunton.

He did not expect to win, but he was determined to create what he called in a letter to his sister 'a rage of enthusiasm' among his supporters. And so he did. One witness of his performance on the hustings said that he had never in his life been so struck by a face as he was by Disraeli's, lividly pale with intensely black eyes blazing from beneath finely arched eyebrows. 'Over a broad, high forehead were ringlets of coal-black, glossy hair, which, combed away from his right temple, fell in luxuriant clusters or bunches over his left cheek and ear, which it entirely concealed from view. There was a sort of half-smile, half-sneer playing about his beautifully-formed mouth, the upper lip of which was curved as we see it in the portraits of Lord Byron. He was very showily attired in a dark bottle-green frock-coat, a waistcoat of the most extravagant pattern, the front of which was almost covered with glittering chains, and in fancy-pattern pantaloons. . . . Altogether he was the most intellectual-looking exquisite I had ever seen.'

High Wycombe High Street. When Disraeli spoke from the portico of the Red Lion (background, right side of street), 'I made them [the whole town] mad. A great many absolutely cried. . . . All the women are on my side.' The thirty-two electors, however, gave only twelve votes to the orator

When he spoke he began 'in a lisping, lackadaisical tone of voice', placing his hands 'in all imaginable positions', 'not because he felt awkward, but apparently for the purpose of exhibiting to the best advantage the glittering rings which decked his white and taper fingers. . . . But as he proceeded all traces of this dandyism and affectation were lost. With a rapidity of utterance perfectly astonishing he referred to past events and indulged in anticipations of the future. The Whigs were, of course, the objects of his unsparing satire, and his eloquent denunciations of them were applauded to the echo. . . . His voice, at first so finical, gradually became full, musical and sonorous, and with every varying sentiment was beautifully modulated. . . . The dandy was transformed . . . into a practised orator.'

He was defeated, as he had expected to be, but he had had an opportunity once more to display his remarkable talents which must surely soon be rewarded. He had also become entangled in a quarrel with Daniel O'Connell, the Irish leader, which spread his fame far beyond the confines of Taunton. He had attacked the Whigs for having formed a parliamentary alliance with O'Connell whom they

Daniel O'Connell, the modern Hercules delivering Ireland from her oppressors. The *Spectator* declared that Disraeli was like a puppy yelping from the kick of a strong-limbed horse when he attacked O'Connell, but others (including himself) were suitably impressed

had formerly 'denounced as a traitor'; and, after reading a garbled version of his attack, O'Connell furiously retaliated by castigating Disraeli as a 'living lie', 'a vile creature', 'a reptile', a man who, by his opportunist conversion to Toryism, had displayed his utter 'perfidy, selfishness, depravity and want of principle'. 'His name shows that he is of Jewish origin,' O'Connell added. 'I do not use it as a term of reproach; there are many most respectable Jews. But there are, as in every other people, some of the lowest and most disgusting grade of moral turpitude; and of those I look upon Mr Disraeli as the worst.'

Disraeli reacted in kind. Unable to challenge O'Connell who, having once killed a man in a duel, had vowed never to fight again, he challenged instead O'Connell's son who had himself once called out Lord Alvanley for insulting his father. When Morgan O'Connell replied that he was not answerable for what his father might say, Disraeli wrote an open letter to Daniel O'Connell for publication in the newspapers, followed by a second letter to the son in which he said he would take every opportunity of holding his father's name 'up to public contempt', and fervently praying that some member of his family would 'attempt to avenge the inextinguishable hatred' with which he would 'pursue his existence'.

The tone of the letters is too ferociously vindictive for modern taste; but they were much admired at the time, and Disraeli proudly told the electors of Taunton that for a month scarcely a day elapsed on which he did not receive congratulatory letters. In his diary he noted that he had greatly distinguished himself.

More truly distinguished, however, was another open letter which he published later in 1835, *A Vindication of the English Constitution in a Letter to a Noble and Learned Lord [Lyndhurst] by Disraeli, the Younger.* This long letter, issued in the form of a book of two hundred pages, set forth the ideas which were to be central to Disraeli's political thought. It attacked the Whigs as an oligarchic, aristocratic party acting against the national interest; it presented the Tories as the country's democratic party, protecting the rights of the common people; it praised the virtues of the country's traditional institutions, particularly the House of Lords and the landed interests which supported it, and poured scorn upon the abstract theories of the doctrinaires, particularly the Utilitarians.

His father was delighted with the *Vindication*. 'You have now a positive *name* and a *being* in the great political world,' he told his son. 'It is for you to preserve the wide reputation which I am positive is now secured.' Lord Lyndhurst was equally pleased with Disraeli's 'masterly' work. Even Peel expressed himself as 'gratified and surprised to find that a familiar and apparently exhausted topic could be treated with so much of original force of argument'.

As a Tory propagandist Disraeli also wrote anonymously for the *Morning Post* a series of articles in which he attacked the government in the most scurrilous terms, anathematizing the Attorney-General, for instance, as a 'base-born Scotchman', a 'booing, fawning, jobbing progeny of haggis and cockaleekie'. In subsequent letters to *The Times*, to whose editor he was introduced by Lyndhurst, Disraeli, under the pseudonym of 'Runnymede', continued his virulent attacks, castigating Melbourne, the 'lounging, sauntering' Prime Minister, and Palmerston, the Foreign Secretary, 'the Lord Fanny of diplomacy', vilifying O'Connell as 'the hired instrument of the Papacy', and O'Connell's countrymen as a 'wild, reckless, indolent, uncertain and superstitious race'.

Even by the standards of the 1830s these virulent assaults were considered strong meat; and some of the fiercer and more libellous phrases were softened by the editor's pencil. But Disraeli, while pretending not to know the identity of 'Runnymede', was well satisfied with the letters' effect. 'Establish my character as a great political writer by the Letters of Runnymede,' he noted in his diary, making a résumé of his progress that year. 'My influence greatly increases from the perfect confidence of [Lyndhurst] and my success as a political writer.'

The success, though, was not financially remunerative; and he had to turn to other forms of writing to make money. He had tried his hand at poetry the year before and had produced the *Revolutionary Epick* which he had read aloud, clothed in the most theatrical costume with red rosettes on his shoes and scent on his hair, at a party at the Austens'. But the reading was not a success; and, after his departure, one of the other guests recited a parody of the lamentable poem which reduced the company to helpless laughter. Sensibly accepting that he was not a poet, Disraeli returned to writing novels and had soon finished a love story, *Henrietta Temple*, which was successful enough to allow him to pay off some of his debts but by no means all. He followed this with *Venetia, or the Poet's Daughter*, a novel partly based on the lives of Byron and Shelley, though placed towards the end of the eighteenth century. This, too, made him some money, but not as much as *Henrietta Temple* and not nearly enough to pay off all his debts.

Before long these debts had risen to over £20,000; and there seemed no way of settling them. There had been a time when he could always borrow from Benjamin Austen, but Austen had come to feel that Disraeli was no longer much interested in him now that he had found other more influential friends in smarter circles. When Disraeli asked for a loan of £1,200 in return for an assignment of his copyrights, Austen replied that, as Disraeli already owed him £300 – which he would not ask to be repaid for the moment – he did not feel able to

Opposite: Lord Lyndhurst, the Tory Lord Chancellor who was Disraeli's greatest political aid and ally in the early years

lend him a further £1,200 and suggested that he should approach his father. Austen's wife eventually persuaded her husband to change his mind; but when the time came to repay the money and Disraeli could not do so, Austen again became sulky and cross, threatening to go to law, until Disraeli was forced at length to appeal to his father. So the debt was repaid. The friendship with the Austens, however, was irrevocably broken, and they were left suffering under what Sir Philip Rose described as 'a morbid feeling of slight and neglect'.

Although the debts to Austen were settled at last, this was far from being the end of Disraeli's financial distress. For a time he was helped by a solicitor, William Pyne, who performed 'singular good services'. But by February 1837 the situation had once more become desperate. His creditors were now so clamorous that he was again reluctantly compelled to appeal to his father to whom he did not care to reveal the full amount of his indebtedness at which, in any case, he could probably hazard no more than a rough guess. In a painful interview at Bradenham he 'ventured to say £2,000 might be required'. But this did not go far. He had to return for more. He was given more. Yet, even so, only the more importunate of the creditors were paid. Other debts still loomed and mounted.

They did not apparently cause Disraeli any excessive worry. It was as though he accepted debts as part of the essential accoutrements of a man of fashion. A character in one of his novels expresses himself as being actually 'fond of his debts', one of 'the two greatest stimulants in the world', the other being youth. What would he be without them? Perhaps Disraeli thought so, too.

Certainly his insolvency interfered little either with his rise in Conservative society or with his political ambitions. And in July 1837, soon after the accession of Queen Victoria, he was at last elected to Parliament as one of the Conservative Members for Maidstone, helped in his defeat of the Radical candidate by the capacious pockets of the other successful Conservative candidate, Wyndham Lewis.

Wyndham Lewis owned land in Wales, a share in a highly profitable ironworks and a handsome house in London. And when he died a few months after his re-election at Maidstone his widow was left a rich woman. Mary Anne Lewis was the daughter of a naval officer who had died when she was a child, leaving her to be brought up in relative poverty in the house of her stepfather at Clifton. To the relief of her family, at the age of twenty-three, she had found a rich husband for herself in Wyndham Lewis and for most of the Regency, and throughout the reigns of George IV and William IV, she had lived contentedly in Wales and London, taking ingenuous pleasure in her position as a hostess able to give large parties to guests of far higher social standing than herself. She was extremely talkative, arch and

capricious, much given to making remarks of guileless absurdity which from other lips might have been considered ironic. On first acquaintance she could appear stupid and tiresome; but those who knew her well were aware of her astuteness. She was capable of deep affection.

On meeting her for the first time Disraeli had found her exasperating. Not that 'insufferable woman', he had protested when asked to take her into dinner. She was a 'pretty little woman', he had admitted on a later occasion; but 'a flirt and a rattle, indeed gifted with a volubility' that must surely have been 'unequalled'. She had told him that she 'liked silent, melancholy men', and he had replied that he had no doubt of it.

Mrs Wyndham Lewis in 1829, ten years before she became Mary Anne Disraeli. 'He is a genius', she recorded when analysing their relationship; 'She is a dunce'

At that time Disraeli had been having an affair with a doctor's wife, Clara Bolton, whose husband seems to have condoned both this liaison and a subsequent one with Sir Francis Sykes whose wife, Henrietta, in turn became Disraeli's mistress.

Disraeli's affair with Lady Sykes had developed into a grand passion. She was an impetuous, sensual woman, good looking, intelligent and warm hearted; and she had fulfilled for him a need for maternal love, admiration, sympathy and comfort that his mother, to whom he had never felt close, had not been disposed to satisfy. 'It is the night Dearest,' she had written to him in one of her passionate letters which cast a clear light on their relationship, 'the night that we used to pass so happily together. I cannot sleep and the sad reality that we are parted presses heavily upon me. . . . I love you. . . . The dear head is it better? That it were pillowed on my bosom for ever. I would be such an affectionate old Nurse to my child and soothe every pain. . . . A thousand and a thousand kisses. Good night. Sleep and dream of – your Mother.'

The affair had caused a good deal of scandal. Sir Francis Sykes, having involved himself with Clara Bolton, was obliged to be complaisant. But Henrietta's father, a rich brewer, had been furious, had cut his daughter when he saw her in the street with her lover – who had been so absorbed in his mistress that he had not noticed the slight – and had threatened to go on cutting them both until their intimacy ceased. In fact, the intimacy had not lasted long; for Henrietta was too possessive and cloying for Disraeli's taste after the first flood of passion had subsided. 'I love you even to madness,' she had written to him when such protestations had become irritating rather than flattering. 'I swear I suffer the torments of the damned when you are away and although there is nothing I would not sacrifice to give you a moment's enjoyment I cannot bear that your amusement should spring from any other source than myself.' It was, therefore, with relief that soon after this letter was written Disraeli learned that Henrietta had been seduced by his friend, the portrait-painter Daniel Maclise; he was thus given an excuse to bring to an end an affair which had become boring and irksome.

After Henrietta Sykes's suffocating possessiveness, Mary Anne Lewis's obvious but far less intense, even playful, affection for him was refreshing. After his initial disdain, he began to grow fond of her. Although at forty-five she was twelve years older than himself, he even started to think of marrying her. He had had passing thoughts of marriage in the past, first to William Meredith's sister – to whom he proposed and from whom he received, without any apparent dismay, a refusal – then to Lady Charlotte Bertie, the very rich daughter of the Earl of Bertie who eventually married the even richer Josiah John

Hyde Park, near the Grosvenor Gate home of Mary Anne Lewis in which Disraeli and his wife were to live

Guest and, after Guest's death, their son's tutor, Charles Schreiber. When mentioning to his sister the possibility of marriage to Lady Charlotte, Disraeli had alluded to the important fact that she had £25,000. 'As for love,' he had added dismissively, 'all my friends who married for love and beauty beat their wives or live apart from them. . . . I may commit many follies in life, but I never intend to marry for "love".'

His friends naturally assumed that when he considered marriage to Mary Anne Lewis he was thinking mainly of her money; and no doubt had she been poor he would not have contemplated her at all. Indeed, he confessed to her himself that when he first made advances to her he 'was influenced by no romantic feelings'. Yet it is clear from the letters he wrote to her, and the poetry he composed for her, that these feelings did come later. When he discovered that she had no more than a life interest in part of her husband's fortune, worth something rather less than £5,000 a year, and that the share in the ironworks had gone to a brother, Disraeli nevertheless continued to press his suit.

Her response was deflating: she would not give an answer until a year after her husband's death. In the meantime she went to stay with her family in Clifton whence few letters arrived in London and those less than gratifying to a suitor. On her return to London he called at

St George's, Hanover Square, where Benjamin and Mary Anne were married

her house in Grosvenor Gate where his insistent demand for a definite answer led to a painful quarrel during which she called him 'a selfish bully' and told him to leave the house and never come back.

He went home to write her an enormous long letter, hurt, resentful, pleading and admonitory. But it was effective. 'For God's sake come to me,' she replied. 'I am ill and almost distracted. I will answer all you wish. . . . I am devoted to you.' Not long afterwards they were married at St George's, Hanover Square, and left for a honeymoon in Tunbridge Wells, Germany and Paris which lasted for two months.

To everyone's surprise they were perfectly happy. She adored him; he treated her with devoted courtesy. 'Dizzy married me for my money,' she used to say. 'But if he had the chance again, he would marry me for love.' 'There was no care which she could not mitigate,' her husband said of her fondly in return, 'and no difficulty which she could not face. She was the most cheerful and the most courageous woman I ever knew.' As the years went by, her unconventional taste, dress, conversation and manners became increasingly eccentric, not to say bizarre. But Disraeli pretended not to notice that there was anything about her that was not both attractive and admirable; and if anyone spoke of her slightingly he came at once to her defence. She responded by giving up her whole life to his. Although he was always reluctant to reveal to her – as he had been to reveal to his father – the full burden of his debts, she settled many for him without complaint. If she were ill or tired she pretended not to be for his sake: once when she trapped her hand in a carriage door she bore the pain in silence lest she worried him before an important speech. Shortly before she died she told a friend that her life had been one long 'scene of happiness, owing to his love and kindness'.

Despite the happy intimacy of his marriage, Disraeli's devotion to his sister was unimpaired; and he continued to write to her those long, detailed, affectionate letters which provide a self-congratulatory chronicle of his early career.

That career in Parliament had got off to a bad start. Determined to make an impressive mark at the outset, he waited scarcely more than a fortnight before rising on 7 December 1837 to deliver a maiden speech which everyone in the House would remember. This was foolhardy enough; but to choose to speak on a subject – the validity of various Irish elections – which was certain to arouse the anger of the Irish Members, whom he had already deeply offended, was even more reckless. Nor was the florid, self-assured manner in which he began calculated to endear him to a House where a certain modest, respectful reticence was traditionally expected of the newly elected. After a few moments Members on both sides began to laugh at him; then, when he continued in what one of them considered as absurd a mixture of 'insolence and folly' as he had ever heard in his life, Disraeli's words were drowned in 'hisses, groans, hoots, catcalls, drumming with feet, loud conversation and imitation of animals'. Eventually he was forced to surrender, shouting above the noise, 'I will sit down now, but the time will come when you will hear me.'

Making light of this disaster in a letter to his sister, Disraeli admitted that his début had been a failure, but 'the failure', he added, 'was not occasioned by my breaking down or any incompetency on my part, but from the physical powers of my adversaries. I can give you no idea how bitter, how factious, how unfair they were.' In a subsequent letter he quoted some sensible advice given him by an experienced Irish Member, R.L. O'Sheil, who did not like O'Connell: 'You have shown to the House . . . that you have an unlimited command of language, that you have courage, temper and readiness. Now get rid of your genius for a session. Speak often, for you must not show yourself cowed, but speak shortly. Be very quiet, try to be dull. . . . Quote figures, dates, calculations. And in a short time the House will sigh for the wit and eloquence which they all know are in you; they will encourage you to pour them forth, and then you will have the ear of the House and be a favourite.'

Disraeli assured both Sarah and his wife that he soon *was* a

favourite. In letter after letter he spoke of his mounting successes. 'Nothing daunted, and acting on the advice of Sheil, I spoke again last night and with complete success. . . . All agree that I managed in a few minutes by my voice and manner to please everyone in the House. . . . I arose and made a most successful speech. Indeed, it was not merely a very good speech, but it was by far, and by all sides agreed, the very best speech of the evening. . . . I have become very popular in the House. . . . I made a most brilliant and triumphant speech last night. . . . I rose with several men at the same time; but the House called for me, and I spoke with great effect and amid loud cheering and laughter. . . . My last speech was very successful, the best *coup* I have yet made. . . . From Sir Robert Peel downwards there is but one opinion of my great success. . . .'

While Disraeli's triumph was not as complete as these letters imply, by the summer of 1841 he had established himself as one of the most gifted speakers on the Tory left, with a strong belief in 'a regenerated Toryism resting on the broad basis of faith in the people', in 'the splendour of the Crown, the lustre of the peerage, the privileges of the Commons, the rights of the poor . . . that magnificent concord of all

Disraeli's romantic attraction to a traditional England, in which a benevolent squirearchy provided pleasantly paternal social support for the poor, helped to make him an opponent of the new Poor Law

interests, of all classes, on which our national greatness and prosperity depends'. He had 'not been ashamed to say' that he wished 'more sympathy had been shown on both sides towards the Chartists'; and that a union 'between the Conservative party and the Radical masses' offered the only means by which the Empire could be preserved.

Having proved his merit, Disraeli felt sure that his chance of office in a Conservative government had come when, in May 1841, the Whigs were defeated on a motion of no confidence and a general election was called. Without the help of Wyndham Lewis's money, he could not meet the greedy demands of the electors at Maidstone; but, despite a campaign waged against him on the subject of his debts, he was elected for Shrewsbury, and waited eagerly for Peel's call to office. He believed that Peel admired him. He had told Sarah how he had been invited to dinner by the Conservative leader and, arriving late, had 'found some 25 gentlemen grubbing in solemn silence'. 'I threw a shot over the table,' he continued, 'and got them going, and in time they became even noisy. Peel, I think was quite pleased that I broke the awful stillness, as he talked to me a good deal, though we were far removed.' It was true that he had occasionally disagreed with official Conservative policy, but Peel had shown no resentment.

Yet the expected invitation did not come. The reason was not surprising. Disraeli was not altogether trusted in the party. The wounds inflicted by his writings were not forgotten; he was believed by

Disraeli was almost alone in his party in his support for the Chartists, if not for their complete programme, when they petitioned Parliament

many to be devious, unreliable, a mischief-maker; the Duke of Rutland thought him 'a designing person'. Besides, Peel had to consider those who had served the party longer than Disraeli had done, as well as those with more influence. Even so, Disraeli was deeply hurt when Peel passed him over. He wrote to him to confess that 'to be unrecognised at this moment' was 'overwhelming' and to appeal to him to save him 'from an intolerable situation'. Mary Anne wrote too. But it was no good. Peel could not give way; and Disraeli felt 'utterly isolated'.

The rebuff was bound to affect his attitude to Peel and ultimately to drive him into opposition to official Conservative policy. It did not do so immediately: for two complete sessions he loyally supported the new government. But after a time he drew closer to a rebellious group within the party known as Young England, a group in opposition to Peel's attempt to strengthen party discipline and dedicated to the view that the territorial aristocracy must come into alliance with the lower classes to resist the manufacturers and the new type of radicals, so different from the romantic radicals of Disraeli's youth. The two principal advocates of Young England were the Hon. George Smythe, a brilliant, profligate, extravagant dilettante; and the Duke of Rutland's son, the less dazzling but extremely handsome, gifted, earnest and good-natured Lord John Manners, Smythe's best friend at Eton and Cambridge. Disraeli, instinctively predisposed to like clever and dissolute young men like Smythe, was welcomed by the group as an important addition to its cause. But not all its members liked or trusted him. Manners wondered whether Disraeli really believed all he said, whether the views he propounded were sincerely held. Alexander Baillie-Cochrane, another of the group's leaders, feared that Disraeli would merely use the group for his own purposes. As Smythe said, Baillie-Cochrane also dreaded Disraeli's jokes and he was never quite sure what thoughts were passing through the devious mind behind that enigmatic face, what true feelings were concealed beneath that ironic yet extravagant manner.

To several of Peel's supporters, worried about the future of a government beset by the seemingly insuperable obstacles created by a continuing economic depression, Disraeli's support of Young England appeared yet another proof of his utter unreliability. Sir James Graham, the Home Secretary, for instance, had now come to the conclusion that he was 'unprincipled' and 'mischievous'. Graham had no longer any desire to keep on good terms with him; 'it would be better for the party if he were driven into the ranks of [its] open enemies'.

Already, in fact, Disraeli had spoken in the House in strong condemnation of various aspects of government policy; and he was

soon to aggravate his unpopularity with the Cabinet both by the publication of one of his best-known political novels, *Coningsby*, in which the Conservatives' recent past was held up to contumely, and by brashly asking the government which he had assailed for its help in acquiring an official appointment for his brother, James. This request, Graham thought, was 'doubly impudent' when one remembered 'his conduct and language in the House of Commons'. Peel thought so, too, but was 'very glad that Mr Disraeli had asked for an office for his brother'; for it was 'a good thing when such a man [put] his shabbiness on record'. 'He asked me for office himself,' Peel added in reply to Graham, 'and I am not surprised that being refused he became independent. . . . But to ask favour after his conduct last session is too bad.'

The author of *Coningsby* flourished in the society receptions, balls and dinners of the late 1840s

Opposite page: Lord John Manners, later Duke of Rutland. André Maurois described him as 'a Lancelot lost in a world of machinery'. Like the other founders of the Young England group, his recognition of the need for Disraeli's leadership overcame his doubts about Benjamin's sincerity: 'Dear Cid and Captain' was their style of address to him in letters

Disraeli stayed frequently at Deepdene, where he wrote *Coningsby* among 'its glades and galleries'. It was the home of the millionaire supporter of Young England, Henry Hope: the novel satisfied the romantic aspirations of the movement (*opposite: above*, Belvoir Castle, called Beaumanoir in *Coningsby*); and it expressed Disraeli's hostility to Peel's 'Conservatism', which rejected the past, offered 'no redress for the Present' and made 'no preparation for the Future'

When Queen Victoria first encountered Disraeli in 1845 at Stowe, seat of the Duke of Buckingham (*opposite: below*), she made no record in her journals; but Mrs Disraeli's singularity *was* noted. '*She* is very vulgar,' the Queen wrote later, 'not so much in appearance as in her way of speaking'

Sybil was intended to illustrate 'the Condition of the People'. 'The Capitalist flourishes, he amasses immense wealth; we sink, lower and lower; lower than the beasts of burthen. . . . And yet they tell us that the interests of Capital and Labour are identical'

The mines. 'Hour after hour elapses, and all that reminds the infant Trappers of the world they have quitted . . . is the passage of the coal-waggons for which they open the air-doors of the galleries'

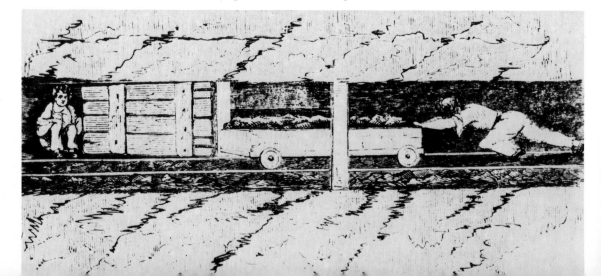

Trying to reach the factory gates on time. *Sybil* indicated how the wage-earning burden was being borne by women and children

In May 1845 *Coningsby* was followed by a sequel, *Sybil*, which presented Peel and his friends in an even more unfavourable light than its predecessor. And after that there appeared little possibility of a reconciliation between Disraeli and the leaders of his party. Nor, evidently, did he hope for one. It seems as if he had by now firmly decided that, at the age of forty, and having spent the past seven of these years in Parliament, he could only achieve the fame, for which he had come to Westminster, by destroying the current leadership of the Conservative party. Having reached that decision, he threw off all restraint. In a series of speeches he poured such scorn upon Peel that the Prime Minister, a shy, awkward man with an aloof manner and an excessive sensitivity to ridicule, was observed more than once to change colour as he listened, to laugh loudly and defensively in pretence of amusement, or to pull his hat down over his eyes and his nervously twitching face.

In the course of these speeches, delivered on any subject from which advantage could be taken of the government's embarrassment, Disraeli perfected a style of speaking which was as effective as it was inimitable.

In earlier years his manner, as displayed catastrophically in his maiden speech, had not always been to the House's taste. He was clever, courageous and original, it was admitted; but it was held against him that there was too much ostentation in the cleverness, that he was too didactic, that his flights of sarcasm were insufficiently tempered by tact. Even now, at the beginning of his speeches, as a contemporary observer recorded, he seemed quite 'indifferent to the trouble of pleasing'. 'With his supercilious expression of countenance ... and a dilettante affectation, he stands with his hands on his hips, or his thumbs in the armholes of his waistcoat, while there is a slight, very slight, gyratory movement of the upper part of his body.... His words are not as much delivered as they flow from the mouth, as if it were really too much trouble for so clever, so intellectual – and in a word, so literary a man to speak at all.'

But then his manner would change and he would become more animated, though still less so than any other speaker of equal power over the House. 'You then can detect the nicest and most delicate inflexions in the tones of his voice; and they are managed, with exquisite art, to give effect to the irony or sarcasm of the moment.... In conveying masked enmities by means of a glance, a shrug, an altered tone of voice, or a transient expression of face, he is unrivalled.... You might consider him wholly unconscious of the effect he is producing; for he never seems to laugh or to chuckle, however slightly, at his own hits. While all around him are convulsed with merriment or excitement at some of his finely-wrought sarcasms, he holds himself, seemingly, in total suspension, as though he had no existence for the ordinary feelings and passions of humanity; and the moment the shouts and confusion have subsided, the same calm, low, monotonous, yet distinct and searching voice, is heard still pouring forth his ideas, while he is preparing to launch another sarcasm, hissing hot, into the soul of his victim.'

He cut up a Minister, another observer said, 'with as much *sang-froid* as an anatomist cuts up a frog'. All contemporaries, indeed, agreed that it was this impassiveness which made his performances in the House so impressive.

When listening to an attack upon himself or his party he would always sit with his legs crossed, his arms folded, his hat pulled down slightly over his eyes, pretending to slumber, betraying emotion when a sentence wounded him only by a slight twist of a foot or a pulling forward of a wrist of his shirt. If an attack were particularly savage he would twist his body round, place his eyeglass to his right eye, glance for about three seconds at the clock over the entrance door, then replace the glass in his breast pocket, and relapse into simulated sleep.

On rising to speak himself, he prepared his fellow Members for his words by smoothing his clothes down over his hips with the palms of his hands, then pulling his coat down in front and throwing his shoulders back. He always began slowly and deliberately, pronouncing each syllable of every word precisely, even pedantically. Occasionally an uncommonly good witticism would be prefaced by an almost apologetic cough as he placed both hands behind his back, produced a white cambric handkerchief in his left, passed it to his right, then brushed the tip of his nose with it before replacing it in his pocket. But his gestures were very few. He had no need of them. The matter and delivery of his speeches were enough to command attention. The matter can still be read, and read with pleasure. But, in the words of Sir William Fraser, Member for Kidderminster and a celebrated Carlton Club raconteur, 'no one who has not [heard Disraeli speak in Parliament] can form any idea of his powers. His speeches when read give no adequate idea of their effect. The impression made on an emotional assembly like the House of Commons can never be put into print.'

When a potato disease caused hardship in southern England and famine in Ireland, and Peel decided to bring forward the repeal of the protective duties on foreign imported grain known as the 'Corn Laws', Disraeli was provided with an ideally controversial measure for the display of his extraordinary gifts – for the proposed repeal of the Corn Laws would naturally provoke fierce resentment among Conservative Members with agricultural interests and might well provoke the split in the party for which Disraeli was hoping.

On 22 January 1846, after long and boring perorations by Peel and the Whig leader Lord John Russell which left the House silent and dispirited, he leapt to the attack with a brilliant speech which transformed the atmosphere, turned the debate into one of principle, constancy, 'independence of party' and 'integrity of public men'. He brought the supporters of protection to their feet and they cheered him enthusiastically for several minutes.

One Member deeply impressed by Disraeli's speech was Lord George Bentinck, a son of the Duke of Portland, who was at that time better known on the turf than he was in the House where he had sat for many years in total silence. A former supporter of Peel, he now regarded him as a traitor to the party, and looked upon Disraeli as the most likely man to bring him down. Disraeli, in turn, realized that Bentinck, to whom he became devoted, was the sort of ally, respected, patrician and extremely well connected, without whose support his ambitions might never be realized.

Between them, Disraeli and Bentinck skilfully presented the case for the Corn Laws, Bentinck by bringing his astonishing memory for

Lord George Bentinck. 'The Jockey and the Jew' – an unfair description, since Bentinck put protectionist politics before his racing interests – worked well together, Bentinck's perseverance making up for his inabilities as a public speaker

Punch praised Peel after his death for repealing the Corn Laws

figures to effective play in the recitation of statistics and by asserting persuasively that the 'proud aristocracy' to which he belonged 'never had been guilty and never could be guilty of double-dealing with the farmers of England'; Disraeli by insisting that agricultural interests in England must always preponderate over manufacturing, and that what those who supported repeal were really after was a transfer of power from the landed classes to the middle-class manufacturers. After one particularly wounding and thunderously acclaimed speech, in which Disraeli had referred emotionally to the people's discontent with 'an inefficient and short-sighted Minister' and to his own 'faith in the primitive and enduring elements in the English character', Peel, who was usually, as Gladstone said, 'altogether helpless in reply', rose angrily to ask why, if Disraeli thought his political career so reprehensible, he had once offered to serve under him.

Rather than ignore this reference to his letter asking for office in 1841, Disraeli, lying with reckless defiance, assured the House that 'nothing of the kind ever occurred', that he had 'never directly or indirectly solicited office'. Peel had the application from Mrs Disraeli's house in his dispatch-case; but, due no doubt to some honourable

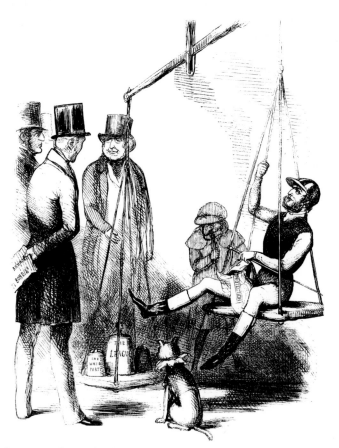

Bentinck became the leader of the protectionists in the Commons: a rather light-weight entrant for the prime ministerial stakes

compunction not to divulge the contents of a private letter, he did not read it out to the House, and Disraeli was spared a damaging and embarrassing disclosure of his dishonesty.

Although 242 of Peel's former supporters were persuaded to vote with Disraeli and Bentinck when the division was taken, the government won with the help of the Whigs and the Radicals; and on 28 May the Corn Law Bill passed its second reading in the Lords.

Disraeli and Bentinck, however, were still determined to drive Peel from office. And they saw their opportunity in what became known as the Irish Coercion Bill, a Bill authorizing a kind of martial law in Ireland where starvation had led to serious disturbances. In continuing his merciless attacks on Peel over the Bill, Bentinck raked up all the errors of the Prime Minister's past to cast furiously in his face; but he could not carry nearly as many Conservatives with him as he had been able to do over the Corn Laws. Over two-thirds of those who had supported him and Disraeli on that issue either abstained or voted with Peel on this one. But the seventy Tories who followed them into the lobby were enough, with the Whigs, Radicals and Irish Members, to defeat the government. A few days later Peel resigned.

The Conservative party, now forced into opposition to a Whig government led by Lord John Russell, seemed irreconcilably split between the supporters of Bentinck and Disraeli, the so-called 'country' Members or protectionists, and those who remained loyal to Peel. The three leaders of these two factions all sat on the Opposition front bench, but never together, Bentinck and Disraeli taking care always to separate themselves from their former leader whose career they had destroyed.

Disraeli's position in the party was wholly transformed. At the general election held in June 1847, about 330 Conservatives were returned, over two-thirds of whom were protectionists; and it was to Disraeli that they were soon obliged to look for leadership. For Bentinck, their nominal leader, was in failing health and was to show that, hard-working and tenacious though he was, he had not the capacity, in Disraeli's privately spoken words, 'to lead an Opposition, still less to lead a Government'. Yet, apart from Disraeli himself, there was no one else of merit to whom the protectionists could turn, all the men with experience of office, or with the qualities required to attain it, being Peelites. 'Disraeli was soon left absolutely alone,' the Duke of Argyll commented, 'the only piece upon the board on that side of politics that was above the level of a pawn. . . . He was like a subaltern in a great battle where every superior officer was killed or wounded.'

Conscious of his new status, Disraeli began to speak and dress for the part. Discarded now were the outlandish clothes of earlier years; and he appeared on the Opposition front bench clothed in winter in a

The Opposition front bench in 1847, rivals pushed together: Peel is second from left, Bentinck and Disraeli second and third from right respectively

dark frock-coat with a double-breasted plush waistcoat, and in summer in a thin plain blue coat, tightly buttoned, with the outlines of 'an unquestionable pair of stays' to be seen through it from the back. He spoke, too, in more measured tones, moderating his few gestures. Aware of the incongruity of his leading a 'country party' when he neither owned a country-house nor represented a country constituency, he began to think of acquiring both. Hughenden Manor, a late eighteenth-century house in Buckinghamshire with some 750 acres, came on to the market at this time for £35,000. He had nothing like enough money to pay for it. Nor had his wife, who had already paid off many of his debts and would have settled others had she known of them. His mother died in April 1847 and his father, now blind, nine months later, so that he had some capital at his disposal at last. But he could not have contemplated the purchase of Hughenden Manor without help from outside his family. He borrowed £5,000 from his solicitors; obtained an overdraft of £14,000 from his bank; and gratefully accepted a loan of £25,000 generously offered to him by Lord George Bentinck and Bentinck's two rich brothers.

Hughenden Manor, as it was when Disraeli bought it in 1852

As the prospective owner of a country estate, Disraeli could now put himself forward as one of the Conservative candidates for the county of Buckingham; and he was elected without a contest. Also returned in the general election of June 1847, as a Liberal for the City of London, was a fellow Jew, Baron de Rothschild. And this was to place Disraeli in an embarrassing position. For, unlike himself, Rothschild was not a convert and was therefore unable to take the parliamentary oath, 'on the faith of a true Christian', which was required of new Members by law. Dependent as they were on Liberal support, the Whigs could be expected to bring in a motion for the removal of the civil disabilities of the Queen's Jewish subjects. And this Russell duly did. His Bill was rejected, however, by the House of Lords; and it was to be several years before Rothschild was able to take part in the proceedings of the Commons.

A few months before Rothschild's election, Disraeli had published his novel, *Tancred*, which contained a passionate vindication of the claims of the Jewish race and a celebration of its destinies. He had propounded the view, which he had long firmly held, that Christianity was Judaism completed and fulfilled. This unorthodox doctrine was certainly not shared by those who supported Russell's motion on the grounds of religious liberty, and was utterly repugnant, not to say, blasphemous, to many Tory Members who considered it their duty to defend the established Church to the last and to deny entry to Parliament to those who, though not Christians, would be entitled to interfere in the Church's organization and doctrine. Yet Disraeli declined to remain silent, as prudence suggested. He knew that his views were unpopular; but he bravely rose to air them all the same, telling the House that 'the very reason for admitting the Jews' was because they could 'show so near an affinity to you', being descended from the people into whose faith Jesus and his disciples were born. 'Where is your Christianity', he asked, 'if you do not believe in their Judaism?'

During his speech there were repeated cries of 'Oh! Oh!', 'and many other signs of general impatience'. And when he sat down there was a cold silence, broken only by shouts of 'Divide! Divide!' It was generally agreed that Disraeli's future prospects had been much harmed: his many critics in the party were given fresh reason to distrust him.

The extent of this distrust was shown only too clearly when Bentinck, who had also spoken in favour of Russell's motion, felt obliged to resign as nominal leader of the protectionists on account of their hostile attitude towards his Whiggishly tolerant views. He had no doubt that Disraeli ought to succeed him. But Lord Derby, as Edward Stanley was soon to become, the leader of the party in the

House of Lords, did not agree. Nor did the Conservative Whips. Instead of Disraeli a compromise was found in the unexceptionable and uninspiring figure of Lord Granby, the Duke of Rutland's heir. Recognizing his own obvious incompetence, Granby soon resigned, though, leaving the appointment vacant.

It was eleven years after Lionel de Rothschild was first elected to the House of Commons that practising Jews were finally admitted and he was at last allowed to take his seat

Disraeli appeared the inevitable choice as his successor, particularly after a marvellous speech ridiculing the performance of a government whose Chancellor of the Exchequer had been obliged to introduce four budgets in six months. His cause was canvassed by several influential supporters, including the Duke of Newcastle and Lord Henry Bentinck, brother of Lord George who died of a heart attack in September 1848. But the prejudice against Disraeli was still too strong. 'I have been warned repeatedly not to trust Disraeli,' wrote one of the Whips to Lord Derby. 'This I conclude is attributable to some circumstances of his earlier life with which I am not familiar, but have little doubt you are.' Besides, if there were to be any hope of a

Disraeli's attitude to protection became increasingly ambivalent, as his judgment of its political value altered. Party labels became more and more confused at the beginning of the 1850s: when Disraeli moved a debate on agricultural distress in early 1850, he found more 'Peelites' on his side than on Peel's

reconciliation with the Peelites, Disraeli would be a liability rather than an asset to the party because they could never forgive him for engineering the fall of their hero.

So – having selected as leader J.C. Herries, a seventy-year-old mediocrity who had served as a Minister in the reign of George IV – Derby wrote to Disraeli to tell him that though the party could not give 'a general and cheerful approval' to his election as leader, he hoped that he would give his 'generous support' to one of inferior abilities who could nevertheless command 'a more general feeling in his favour'. Disraeli did not in the least care to do so. He replied that he did not want to sacrifice his health, a happy home and interesting pursuits for a political career which could bring him 'little fame'. He would prefer, he added, to act 'alone and unshackled'. Alarmed by this veiled threat, and encouraged by Herries who did not want to be leader on his own, Derby now urged Disraeli to agree to a kind of triumvirate which would include Herries and Granby as well as himself. Realizing that this solution was quite impractical and that he would naturally emerge in time as the effective leader, Disraeli accepted it. And within a year he was the acknowledged leader of the Opposition in the House of Commons.

He had taken the first major step towards power; but the Conservatives were still a long way from office – for the Liberals, Radicals, Irish and Peelites could usually be relied upon to support the Whig government whenever the danger of the Tory alternative seemed too threatening. In the meantime Disraeli skilfully made for himself a reputation as a sound supporter of what he termed 'the aristocratic settlement of the country', which he was careful to explain did not mean the rule of the selfish, theorizing Whig grandees, with their metropolitan houses and cosmopolitan tastes, but that of the territorial aristocracy of the broad counties of England who were the mainstay of English freedom, the natural protectors of the people of a country which was 'the only important European community still governed by traditionary influences', and which, alone 'amid the shameless wreck of nations', had 'maintained her honour, her liberty, her order, her authority, and her wealth'.

While propagating this philosophy, so attractive to the country Members, Disraeli worked hard; assiduously studying the records of past sessions; constantly looking for issues – now that he had come to the conclusion that protection was no longer a policy worth pursuing – that would earn the Conservatives the nation's attention and respect; taking care to show that the depth of the social concern that informed his novel *Sybil* was a genuine feeling by warmly supporting Lord Ashley's new Factories Bill; less commendably coming to the support of the landed interest in general, and of Lord Londonderry in particular, by speaking against a Bill proposing official inspection of coal-mines; looking out eagerly for any issue on which the Whig government might be brought down.

Such an opportunity occurred in the autumn of 1850 when the Pope – having issued a brief dividing England into twelve bishoprics and having appointed Nicholas Wiseman as Archbishop of Westminster – announced that the English people, so long severed from Rome, were about to rejoin the Holy Church.

On his own initiative, and to use Disraeli's phrase, 'indulging in his hereditary foible [by] having a shy at the Papists', Russell appointed himself the Protestants' champion, violently attacked the Pope's aggression and cast a few wild, glancing blows at those High Church Anglicans, the Puseyites, whom he considered little better than the Papists themselves. The consequences of this attack were catastrophic for Russell: he immediately lost not only the support of the Irish Members but also of the Peelites, several of whom were High Churchmen and most of whom deplored Russell's intolerance. In

Lord John Russell's vigorous attack on the Pope and 'the danger within the gates from the unworthy sons of the Church of England herself' was followed the next day, 5 November, by the burning of effigies of the Pope and Cardinal Wiseman, Archbishop of Westminster. But the policy was ill advised politically, for he had alienated not only the Irish MPs but also English High Churchmen, and he lost office as a consequence

February 1851 he felt obliged to resign after an adverse vote, and Lord Derby was required by the Queen to form a government.

That Disraeli would have to be a member of this government was not in doubt. But the Queen did not in the least relish the thought. She had never at all liked the sound of Mr Disraeli, and her low opinion of him had been confirmed by his conduct towards Sir Robert Peel who had died a few months before. She accepted Disraeli, she told Derby, on condition that the Prime Minister would be responsible for his conduct. Should she have cause to be displeased with him when in office, she added, she would remind Derby 'of what had now passed'. Derby 'promised to be responsible', so the Prince Consort noted, 'and excused [Disraeli] for his former bitterness by his desire to establish his reputation for cleverness and sharpness; nobody had gained so much by Parliamentary schooling and he had of late quite changed his tone.'

Although Disraeli was willing to serve in a government under Derby, few other competent men could be found to join them. William Ewart Gladstone, who had served both as President of the Board of Trade and Secretary for War under Peel, was offered any department he cared to name, apart from the Foreign Office; but, like all the other Peelites, Gladstone, as Disraeli recorded, 'declined to act unless the principle of Protection were unequivocally renounced'. Henry Goulburn, who had been Peel's Chancellor of the Exchequer, was equally uncooperative. In desperation Derby turned to relatively obscure men whose names were quite unfamiliar to most people outside the House. One of these was Sir Robert Inglis, Member for

Oxford University, a confusing and clumsy speaker who had gained for himself a certain notoriety by announcing to the House – in the course of a rambling complaint that the wife of a certain prisoner in his constituency had not been allowed free access to go in and out of prison to visit her husband – that things had come 'to a pretty pass in this country when an Englishman, [could] not have his wife backwards and forwards'. During the subsequent shouts of laughter which had echoed round the House even Peel had been observed to lose 'his habitual self-control and lean down his head in convulsions'.

The unfortunate butt of this merriment was now offered the Board of Control. Another Member of doubtful competence, Henry Corry, was offered a seat in the Cabinet, whereupon, Disraeli said, the poor man did not actually faint but turned very pale before refusing. Lord Ellenborough was asked to become Lord Privy Seal, a post which he accepted 'but, having been sent on a mission to Mr Goulburn in order to see whether he could convert him,' so the Prince Consort recorded, 'he came home himself converted, and withdrew his acceptance'. Then, at a meeting of potential Ministers in Derby's house, J. W. Henley, the Member for Oxfordshire, whom Derby scarcely knew, was offered the Board of Trade. But, after sitting for a time on a chair in the dining-room with an expression at once astonished and morose on his crabbed face, as Disraeli described him, 'leaning with both hands on an ashen staff, and with the countenance of an ill-conditioned Poor Law Guardian censured for some act of harshness', he flatly refused to consider it. Old J. C. Herries, who it was hoped would become Chancellor of the Exchequer, kept mumbling about not having received his summons earlier, and complaining of all the difficulties that would be placed in his way. He did not actually refuse the office but would not say definitely that he accepted it.

So, what had begun in confusion ended in farce. Derby withdrew from the tiresome meeting and, making a sign to Disraeli to join him, spoke to him alone at the far end of the room.

'This will never do!' he said; and after a few other 'remarks on the extraordinary scene he returned to the table. There was silence and he gave it as his opinion that it was his duty to decline the formation of a government . . . from his inability to find Members of the House of Commons who were prepared to cooperate with him . . . [William] Beresford [the Chief Whip] frantically rushed forward and took Lord Derby aside, and said there were several men he knew waiting at the Carlton expecting to be sent for, and implored Lord Derby to reconsider his course. Lord Derby inquired impatiently, "Who was at the Carlton?" Beresford said, "Deedes." "Pshaw!" exclaimed Lord D.' Later that evening he wrote to the Queen to confess his failure; and Russell was back in office – but not for long. A few months later he felt compelled to dismiss Palmerston, his Foreign Secretary, for having high-handedly given his approval to Louis Napoleon's *coup d'état* without troubling to inform either the Queen or the Prime Minister. And, deprived of Palmerston's support, Russell could not survive. Defeated in a vote in which Palmerston joined with Disraeli, Russell resigned again; and Derby made a fresh effort to form a government. By deciding to waste no time in negotiation with the Peelites, and by selecting a majority of its members from the House of Lords, he managed at this second attempt to form a Cabinet.

It was not, however, a very impressive one. Most of the peers were included because of their families rather than their personal qualities, while some of the other Ministers were so little distinguished that, during the course of some Member's speech in the House of Lords, the deaf old Duke of Wellington was heard impatiently and loudly repeating, '*Who? Who?*' as Lord Derby recited his list of unfamiliar names. There was one name that was familiar, though, and that was that of the Chancellor of the Exchequer, Benjamin Disraeli, whose merits, so Sarah Disraeli was assured by her brother, had been recognized by the Duke several years before.

Disraeli had not wanted this particular appointment. Nor had it been well received. Gladstone thought that Disraeli could not have been worse placed. But it seems that the Queen raised objections to his having one of the other senior appointments as these would have inevitably brought the objectionable man more closely into contact with her than would be necessary if he were Chancellor.

At first all went reasonably well. Disraeli, who was Leader of the House of Commons as well as Chancellor, naturally made mistakes owing to his inexperience and his unfamiliarity with the routine of his department. Nor could he avoid inflicting wounds by the sharply sarcastic wit with which he responded to the blunter darts of his opponents. But the mistakes were few; the wounds eventually healed; and even the diarist Charles Greville, by no means predisposed in his favour, conceded that Disraeli had got off to an excellent start.

In December 1852, however, he had to produce an important budget; and this, not entirely due to his own fault, proved his undoing. His decisions to reduce the malt tax and the duties on hops and tea aroused little opposition. But when he came to alter the rates and limits of income tax and to raise the house tax he underestimated both the technical difficulties and the political implications. His budget became even more controversial when he was presented with service estimates far higher than he had been expecting. This entailed a good deal of tinkering with his figures, and not surprisingly provoked a complaint to the Prime Minister about his having to change all his dispositions 'on the very eve of battle'.

'Put a good face on it,' Derby airily replied, 'and we shall pull through. L'audace – l'audace – toujours l'audace!'

This carefree advice was no comfort to Disraeli who rose on 3 December, feeling ill and depressed after an attack of influenza, to make his speech to a House which Greville described as being 'crowded to suffocation'. It was an extremely long speech – lasting for five hours – and a very tedious one, impatiently received. Two members of the Opposition in particular, one a former Chancellor whom Disraeli had derided when on the other side of the House, 'kept interchanging signs, and nudging one another,' so an observer noticed, 'laughing occasionally while Disraeli was speaking; in fact, turning him into ridicule'. Macaulay, who listened more respectfully and thought Disraeli's exposition 'lucid', nevertheless complained that the speech was 'much too long' and that he himself 'could have said the whole as clearly, or more clearly in two hours'. For, after all, Macaulay added, Disraeli's plan was essentially 'nothing but taking the money out of the pockets of the people in towns and putting it into the pockets of growers of malt'.

This was a rather crude verdict; but there was no doubt that, as another observer commented, 'the Budget presented too many

Disraeli wrote to Lady Londonderry after Louis Napoleon's *coup d'état*, giving his analysis of why Lord John Russell should resign. He had been introduced to this socially influential Tory aristocrat by her stepson (and his friend) Lord Castlereagh in 1835 and over many years they discussed matters political – and sometimes not so political ('I don't know what you mean by passing "so much" of my time with Lady Londonderry', he had to protest to Mary Anne before their marriage)

Despite his deafness, his
moodiness and his
hypochondria, Lytton was
one of the more attractive
political figures of the
confused and complacent
1850s

assailable points to have much chance of being adopted'. And so it proved. In the long debates that followed, the Opposition scored heavily over the government's supporters, only Spencer Walpole, the Home Secretary, and Edward Lytton Bulwer, who had assumed the surname Lytton on his mother's death, making speeches of any conviction; while Herries, the financial expert on their side, sat in gloomy, sulky silence, refusing to speak in defence of a budget which he evidently thought ought to have been presented by himself.

Fearful of the consequences of the government's ineptitude and dismayed by the thought of losing office so soon after acquiring it, Disraeli endeavoured to make a deal with the Radicals; but John Bright, summoned to Grosvenor Gate, was rather shocked by the overture, and noted afterwards that Disraeli seemed 'unable to comprehend the morality of our political course'.

Left to defend himself as best he could, Disraeli stood up to speak on the seventh evening of the debate at nearly half past ten during a theatrically violent thunderstorm. It was an appropriately dramatic speech. Gladstone, who considered the budget sadly marred by 'fundamental faults of principle', had to admit that Disraeli's defence of it was 'grand'; it was 'the most powerful' speech he had ever heard from him. 'At the same time it was disgraced by shameless personalities and otherwise.' Gladstone thought that Disraeli had had too much to drink before making it; and this would certainly account for some of the tasteless jokes and jibes which it contained. However, it received a deafening ovation from the government benches.

The uproar grew even louder when Gladstone stood up to speak in reply. Disraeli's speech had been expected to be the last in the debate; and the impropriety of an ordinary Member presuming to follow the Leader of the House angered the Tory Members as much as the realization that their impending defeat would be due to the continuing and inveterate bitterness of the Peelites. At first Gladstone could not make himself heard; but when the hubbub subsided, he delivered himself of a severe rebuke of Disraeli's refusal yet to learn 'the limits of discretion, of moderation, and forbearance that ought to restrain the conduct and language of every member of the House'. He then followed this reprimand with a clever and thorough denunciation of every aspect of the budget. It was a speech which not only ensured the defeat of the government but marked the beginning of that long duel between Gladstone and Disraeli which was to continue for thirty years.

Disraeli listened to it, pale and impassive in the gaslight as if indifferent to its import; and when the vote was taken and the government was defeated and resigned, he merely commented to a colleague that it would be nasty weather for the journey to Osborne.

'After all, Mr. Bright, we both know very well what brings you and me here: ambition.' John Bright, at least ostensibly, put principle first

The young man who had declared, 'Poetry is the safety-valve of my passions, but I wish to act what I write', had still not satisfied his worldly ambitions

The next Monday, at the instigation of Spencer Walpole who passed on a message from Russell, Disraeli made a graceful apology for the rude things he had said in his speech, and expressed his 'grateful thanks for the indulgent . . . the generous manner' in which he had been supported by Members of both sides of the House in attempting to conduct its business. The bland words, spoken with what Lord Morley described as 'infinite polish and grace', did not conceal from his friends the deep disappointment which he felt at being thrown into an exclusion from office that was to last for over five years.

For Disraeli these were frustrating years. His name and features were now well known throughout the country. Journalists constantly referred to him in the newspapers; two biographies of him were shortly to be published; engravings of his portraits frequently appeared in magazines; there was a wax effigy of him in Madame Tussaud's exhibition. Yet he seemed as far as ever from achieving that lasting fame for which he had, as he confessed, gone to Westminster. And there seemed no imminent prospect of winning it. The coalition government, led by the Peelite, Lord Aberdeen, which had come hesitantly into office after the resignation of Lord Derby, looked temptingly weak. But Derby showed little inclination to bring it down, and to undertake so soon the wearisome process of returning again to office himself. 'As a leader of a Party, he is more hopeless than ever!' one of Disraeli's bright young friends, Lord Henry Lennox, was soon to write. 'Devoted to Whist, Billiards, Racing, Betting, making a fool of himself with either Ladies Emily Peel or Mary Yorke. Bulwer Lytton came to Bretby [Lord Chesterfield's country-house] for 3 days and was in despair! Not a word could he extract from Derby about Public affairs.'

Disraeli had the same experience when he went to Derby's country-house, Knowsley, for the first time. Socially it was a perfectly agreeable visit; but, as another guest noticed, Derby seemed 'much bored' when Disraeli wanted to talk politics. The trouble was that – having reformed the party organization and helped to found a new party newspaper, the *Press*, to which he contributed leading articles virulently attacking Aberdeen who, 'crossed in his Cabinet', insulted the House of Lords and plagued his colleagues 'with the crabbed malice of a maundering witch' – Disraeli wanted to attack the government in the House repeatedly and vigorously. In the past an Opposition had been inclined to consider the various proposals of the government then in office on their individual merits. But this was not Disraeli's way. In his strongly held opinion, an Opposition should always be on the attack, constantly on the alert for the weakness that could surely be found in any proposed measure. This belligerent attitude was not in the least to the taste of Derby, who thought the government would fall to pieces before long anyway if left to itself and who appreciated that Disraeli's tactics might make it impossible for them to co-operate with those upon whose help in forming a government they would eventually have to rely.

The relationship between the two men deteriorated sharply when the mismanagement of the Crimean War brought about the fall of Aberdeen's government. The Queen sent for Derby. But Derby told her that he could not hope to form a government without Palmerston, for whom the 'whole country cried out as the only man fit for carrying on the war with success'. And, since Palmerston would not collaborate with Derby, Palmerston himself became Prime Minister – to the utter disgust of Disraeli who not only castigated Derby for

The Crimean War, in which
Florence Nightingale played so
noble a part, was so grossly
mismanaged that Disraeli was given
ample excuse to attack the
government vehemently: 'We seem
to have fallen into another
Walcheren Expedition, and in my
opinion the Ministers ought to be
impeached'

missing a great opportunity but derided Palmerston as 'an impostor,
utterly exhausted, and at the best only ginger beer and not champaign
and now an old painted Pantaloon, very deaf, very blind, and with
false teeth, which would fall out of his mouth when speaking, if he did
not hesitate and halt so in his talk.'

The old impostor nevertheless conducted the war with energy and
confidence, as Disraeli himself ultimately felt bound to acknowledge.
Yet after the fall of Sebastopol, Disraeli saw an opportunity for
attacking Palmerston's policy which seemed bent on unconditional
surrender. In the *Press* he advocated peace; and this drew a sharp
reprimand from Derby who told him that they could not 'with honour
or even with regard to party interests' constitute themselves 'a peace
Opposition merely because they had a war Ministry'.

By this time Disraeli had made himself more unpopular than ever
with certain sections of the party, particularly with readers of the *Press*
who rarely saw Derby's name mentioned, so Lord Malmesbury said,

or, indeed, the name of anyone except Disraeli whom it praised 'in the most fulsome manner'. 'As to Disraeli's unpopularity,' Malmesbury continued in a letter to Derby after a discussion about it with the Chief Whip, 'I see it and regret it; and especially regret that he does not see more of the party in private.'

Tired and dispirited, Disraeli decided to go abroad with Mary Anne, first to take the waters at Spa, then for a holiday in Paris. Refreshed on his return, he resumed his attacks, looking for new sticks with which to beat the government, entering into a secret alliance with a young attaché at the Paris Embassy who passed on to him confidential information which could be used against the Foreign Office, sniping at the Treasury's financial policy, and protesting against 'meeting atrocities by atrocities' in India during the Mutiny of 1857–58. It was not until the beginning of 1858, however, that Palmerston made a calamitous error which rendered his government defenceless. He had already endangered it by appointing the disreputable Lord Clanricarde, a friend of his wife, Lord Privy Seal. But this outrageous appointment might have been lived down had he not tightened up the laws against the illicit manufacture of explosive devices after a bomb made in Birmingham had been used in an attempt by an Italian to kill the French Emperor in Paris. Accused of weakly giving way to French demands that England should cease giving shelter and assistance to assassins, Palmerston was defeated at last. Derby, realizing that unless he accepted office now the 'Conservative party would be broken up for ever', undertook to form a

Viscount Palmerston by Frederick Cruikshank, *c.* 1855. Disraeli later said that it had been easy to settle affairs with Palmerston, 'because he was a man of the world, and was therefore governed by the principle of honor'

government and once more appointed Disraeli Chancellor of the Exchequer.

Yet again Disraeli was not to hold the office for long. Outnumbered in the Commons, the Conservatives could hope to survive only as long as their opponents failed to coalesce in throwing them out. And in 1859 an issue was found which brought the Opposition together and which prompted Palmerston and Russell to agree to serve under whichever one of them might be sent for by the Queen if the government were to be defeated. This issue was the cause of Italian unification. Both Palmerston and Russell were passionately pro-Italian; so were most people in the country. Derby, the Prime Minister, and Lord Malmesbury, the Foreign Secretary, however, were supposed to be, like the Queen, more in favour of the Austrians whose dominions then included those wide tracts of northern Italy which the Italian patriots were intent on wresting from them with the help of the French Emperor. Disraeli, for his part, as Lord Blake has written in his outstanding biography, 'was never much interested in the rights of oppressed nations struggling to be free. Their cause left him cold, and for all his talk about "race", he simply did not understand nationalism. But he was not the man to disregard public opinion.' He urged Derby to resist some pro-Austrian modifications to the Queen's speech which the Queen herself had suggested. Derby did so. But the strength of the combined Opposition could not be resisted. The government was defeated; Palmerston, to the Queen's distress, became Prime Minister once more; and Disraeli was again dispatched into the shadows for a further six long years.

His stock with the party was now extremely low. He was held largely responsible for the defeat of a leader to whom he was accused of being disloyal; and consequently came in for much abuse. Several dissidents in the party followed the example of Lord George Bentinck's cousin, 'Big Ben' Bentinck, the Member for Norfolk, and invariably referred to Disraeli as 'the Jew'. Alexander Beresford Hope, proprietor of the *Saturday Review*, ensured that his journal maintained a consistently hostile tone towards him. Hope's brother-in-law, Lord Robert Cecil, accused Disraeli in an article in the *Quarterly Review* of having but one guiding principle and that was to 'crush the Whigs by combining with the Radicals; he had never led the Conservatives to victory as Sir Robert Peel had led them to victory; he had never procured the triumphant assertion of any Conservative principle'; his one success had been in conducting an Opposition 'so flexible' and 'so shameless', that, 'so long as his party backed him, no government was strong enough to hold out against his attacks'.

Well aware of the extent of the feeling against him, Disraeli offered to resign a leadership 'to which fourteen years of an unqualified

Disraeli watches Palmerston
speaking in the House of Commons
in 1860

devotion [had] not reconciled the party'. This letter, as no doubt
intended, caused the utmost dismay: Conservatives might not all agree
in liking or trusting Disraeli; but they could not do without him.
'When the pinch comes,' one of his supporters advised him,
'notwithstanding their murmuring and cavil, [the party] come to the
scratch like men. . . . I do not think you are sensitive to attacks from our
enemies; do not be too susceptible to the follies of our friends.' By such
persuasion Disraeli was prevailed upon to withdraw his resignation.

Thereafter, though, he was careful to behave with circumspection
towards his critics. And while acting as an energetic Opposition
leader in the House of Commons, speaking regularly in debates, never
allowing Ministers to relax, he abandoned all thought of alliances with
the Radicals and obediently complied with the policy advocated by
Derby who maintained that the tactics to be adopted against the
government must be designed to keep 'the cripples on their legs'.

Unlike Gladstone – whose strong feelings on the Italian question had led him to join the Liberal party and to accept the post of Chancellor of the Exchequer under Palmerston – Disraeli required regular periods of rest from hard work; and when the parliamentary sessions ended he travelled thankfully to Hughenden where he enjoyed strolling about the estate examining all the trees which he loved and many of which he had himself planted. After his walks he would settle down in his library where he had installed those of his father's books which he had chosen to preserve with his own; or he would sit on the terrace 'surveying the peacocks', as he put it; or go down to the lake to see the swans, or to fish. He rarely bothered to fish, though. He dressed like a squire in the country, and he performed the usual duties of a squire; but he never looked like a squire, and he never took to the sports of a squire. For him the pleasures of hunting, shooting and fishing were not to be compared with a walk through the beechwoods with Mary Anne beside him in a pony-cart.

They remained devoted to each other; and would have been perfectly content to stay at Hughenden alone. But such isolation could not be considered. They had to have guests to stay with them, which Disraeli thought was 'as hard work as having a playhouse or keeping an inn'. And they had to visit other houses, 'to feel the pulse of the

Peace at Hughenden: in garden, library or park. A series of contemporary photographs

Raby: 'a real castle . . . the general effect feudal and Plantagenet'

The monument to Isaac D'Israeli, who had died in Tita's arms in 1848, erected by Mary Anne Disraeli at Hughenden fifteen years later

ablest on all the questions of the day'; and this he liked no better than entertaining at home because there was so little to do in strange houses and so much to eat. Occasionally there was the enjoyment of being with children, of whom he was fond; and sometimes there was the pleasure of meeting some such bright, entertaining, refreshing young man as Montagu Corry, who was to become his devoted secretary and confidant, or Lord Dalmeny, the future Earl of Rosebery, both of whom he met at Raby, the Duke of Cleveland's castle.

At Raby, Dalmeny had been amused to hear Disraeli pay one of his elaborately graceful compliments to the Duchess who apologized for being out riding when her guests arrived: 'The pleasure of seeing Your Grace in your riding habit makes up for the loss of your society.' Dalmeny had been even more amused, and touched, at dinner when, having asked Mrs Disraeli if she cared for politics, she replied, 'No I have no time. I have so many books and pamphlets to read and see if his name is in any of them! And I have everything to manage and write his stupid letters. I am sorry when he is in office for then I lose him altogether, and though I have many people who call themselves friends, yet I have no friend like him.'

Also devoted to Disraeli was another eccentric lady, Mrs Brydges Willyams, an elderly widow of Jewish descent whom he had met after she had written various letters to him praising his achievements and referring to their common ancestry. Mr and Mrs Disraeli often went to stay at Torquay, where Mrs Brydges Willyams lived, taking rooms at

Mrs Brydges Willyams, sketched in 1853

A Sketch taken at Torquay Devon in 1853

Mrs Brydges Willyams of Braddon Hill Torquay Devon.

the Royal Hotel, and spending the afternoons and evenings at her house, Mount Braddon. And when they were parted Disraeli wrote regular letters to her, entrancing dispatches, amusing, detailed and consistently entertaining, which throw fascinating sidelights upon Disraeli's social and parliamentary life.

When she died in 1863, Mrs Brydges Willyams left him rather more than £30,000. Even this sum did not enable him to pay off all his debts; but after Andrew Montagu, a Yorkshire landowner, who had enquired at party headquarters how he could best help the Conservative cause, had also come to his assistance, his financial position was much more stable, and the Disraelis' joint income, which had risen to about £9,000 in 1866, allowed them to live with every comfort.

As well as being regular guests in the great country-houses of England, both Whig and Tory, the Disraelis were now also often guests at Windsor. Persuaded by his less aggressive manner in opposition and by the respectful, carefully composed and informative reports which he had written to her when Leader of the House of Commons, the Queen had grown to think that she might have misjudged Disraeli. And when he paid a hyperbolic tribute to the Prince Consort on his untimely death, and assured the widow that his acquaintance with the Prince was 'one of the most satisfactory incidents of his life', her more favourable opinion of him was confirmed for ever. He was invited to the Prince of Wales's wedding; and a month later was granted the honour of a personal audience.

'Mr Disraeli(!) *high office*', Queen Victoria (*right*, at Windsor with Princess Louise) had exclaimed when he had asked for office under Peel. After Prince Albert's death they grew much closer. The Queen responded to Disraeli's sympathetic understanding of her grief; and he was invited to attend the wedding of the future Edward VII at Windsor in 1863 (*opposite*)

The Derby Cabinet of 1866. 'The truce of parties is over', Disraeli wrote after the death of Palmerston. 'I foresee tempestuous times, and great vicissitudes in public life'

These marks of royal favour played their due part in improving Disraeli's reputation in the Conservative party, which noted also his election to Grillions, to the Athenaeum and to a Trusteeship of the British Museum. And when, in October 1865, Palmerston died, and his successor, Russell, brought in an ill-framed Reform Bill which was condemned by some for going too far and by others for not going far enough, Disraeli's skill in helping to bring about Russell's resignation was widely admired.

In June 1866 Derby formed his third Cabinet, in which Disraeli became Chancellor of the Exchequer yet again. It was a far stronger Cabinet than Derby had been able to assemble in the past; and Disraeli, who had played a leading part in the choice of Ministers, including that of Derby's son as Foreign Secretary, was acknowledged to be its dominant member.

The most urgent problem which the new government had to face was that of Reform, the extension of the franchise to a more representative section of the community. Up till now Disraeli's attitude towards Reform had been largely dictated by his determination to force the Whigs out of office. It was now largely dictated by a determination to stay in office himself.

The question of Reform could clearly no longer be shelved or ignored. Derby, who would have preferred to do nothing about it, was convinced by the strength of feeling in the country that the matter would have to be settled. And Disraeli was equally convinced that the matter would have to be seen to be settled by the Conservatives: any idea of a settlement in co-operation with other parties would be fatal. When the Queen offered to intercede with the Liberals he quickly condemned the 'royal project of gracious interposition' as a 'mere phantom', the 'murmuring of children in a dream'. The Conservatives must take the initiative, ride on the surf to shore and land in the leading boat. As it happened, this entailed bringing in a far more wide-ranging Bill than either Derby or Disraeli would have liked; but it did 'dish the Whigs', which is how Disraeli, borrowing a phrase of Derby's, is said to have described his principal object all along. In later years Disraeli attempted to demonstrate that he had consistently had this goal in view, that his recurrent retreats had been advances towards that goal, and that his skilful negotiation of crisis after crisis had been in accordance with a predetermined policy rather than improvised to meet the needs of the hour. In fact, he was consistent only in his determination to bring in a Bill which would leave the government in

Whatever Disraeli's motives, some people at least expected him to push Reform through

At the top of the greasy pole at last. 'A proud thing for a Man "risen from the people" – to have attained!', wrote Queen Victoria; Disraeli's father, she commented, had been not only a Jew, but a 'mere man of letters'

power and the Opposition in disarray. But he achieved this with such marvellous parliamentary skill, such masterly improvisation, that the Reform Bill of 1867 established Disraeli as the hero of the party, which he had always wanted to be.

He returned home in the early hours of 13 April, delighted by the cheers which had greeted a splendid speech and by a decisive vote that had ensured the government's success. He called in at the Carlton Club where a member rose in the crowded dining-room to propose a toast to the man who 'rode the race' and 'did the trick!' He was cheered again and pressingly invited to sit down and join the celebrations. But he hated clubs, as he once confessed, male society never having been much to his taste. Besides, he wanted to get home to his wife. He found her, as he had expected, waiting up for him. She had ordered him his favourite pie and a bottle of champagne. 'Why, my dear,' he said to her with deep affection, 'you are more like a mistress than a wife.'

There could be no doubt now that, after the departure of Lord Derby, Disraeli would succeed him as leader of the Conservative party, or that his succession could be long delayed. Derby had been suffering from successive and increasingly agonizing attacks of gout for several years, and at the beginning of 1868 his doctors told him that he could not hope to recover unless he gave up the burden of office. He wrote to Disraeli to ask him if he were ready to take over. Disraeli replied, without too strict a regard for truth, that he had 'never contemplated nor desired' the office of Prime Minister but that he would 'not shrink from the situation'. So Derby told the Queen that Disraeli, and Disraeli only, 'could command the cordial support *en masse* of his present colleagues'. The Queen gratefully accepted the advice; and so at last Disraeli had, as he put it to friends who congratulated him, 'climbed to the top of the greasy pole'.

There were those in the party, of course, who did not welcome the ascent. Lord Chelmsford, dismissed as Lord Chancellor, crossly complained that it had made the man '*dizzy*'. Lord Cranborne, to become Prime Minister himself as Lord Salisbury, expressed the opinion that Disraeli was an adventurer, a 'mere political gamester' and, as he had 'good cause to know . . . without principles and honesty'. 'In an age of singularly reckless statesmen,' Cranborne added, 'he is I think beyond question the one who is least restrained by fear or scruple.' Derby himself, though, was much more generous, and more in tune with the general feeling in the party, when, in replying to a letter in which Disraeli undertook never to take an important step without consulting him, he expressed the hope that his successor would long continue to retain the position which he had 'fairly and most honourably won'.

The Queen was delighted. 'The present Man will do well,' she assured her eldest daughter, 'and will be particularly loyal and anxious to please me in every way. He is vy. peculiar, but vy. clever and sensible and vy. conciliatory . . . full of poetry, romance and chivalry. When he knelt down to kiss my hand wh. he took in both his – he said: "In loving loyalty and faith."'

This was the secret of Disraeli's success with her. Behind the calculating knowledge that the Queen's support could be of great value to him and the outrageous flattery which led him to assure her, for instance, that nothing in his life had ever been so interesting as his 'confidential correspondence' with one 'so exalted and so inspiring', there lay a genuine romantic attachment to the throne. Having sent her the collected edition of his novels and received in return *Leaves from the Journal of Our Life in the Highlands*, he may have said to her, 'We authors, Ma'am'; he certainly said to Matthew Arnold, 'You have heard me called a flatterer, and it is true. Everyone likes flattery; and, when you

The Fenian outrages and Irish
religious divisions helped Gladstone
to speed Disraeli out of the office he
had so recently won

come to royalty, you should lay it on with a trowel.' But he never
underestimated the Queen's astuteness; he was genuinely fond of her;
in treating her with elaborate courtesy he was behaving towards her as
he did towards all women he liked; in writing her those long, amusing,
informative letters he was indulging a whim to please her rather than
performing a necessary and arduous duty. The Queen understood this,
was touched and grateful.

Looming beyond the pleasant horizons seen from Windsor,
however, was the stern and handsome face of Mr Gladstone. During
the debates on the Reform Bill, Gladstone, outflanked and defeated in
debate, had so often been reduced to angry silence that it became
customary in an age devoted to riddles to ask why Gladstone was like a
telescope and to answer, 'Because Disraeli draws him out, sees through
him and shuts him up.'

But Gladstone was now to get his own back. During 1868 the
bombings of the Fenians, revolutionaries intent upon overthrowing
British rule in Ireland, had reached such a pitch that the government
felt compelled to make some concessions to their cause. So, it being
then considered that the Irish problem was fundamentally a religious
one, the government began to discuss the difficulties facing the Church

in Ireland and the possibility of supporting a Roman Catholic University in Dublin. These discussions had not gone far, however, when Gladstone brought them to a sudden halt by announcing in Parliament that the Anglican Establishment in Ireland ought to be abolished altogether. This proved an issue on which the Liberal party could be united and on which Disraeli, though he made a fine speech in favour of Establishment, could accordingly be defeated. After an adverse vote and a subsequent general election, Disraeli was forced to resign. His few months as Prime Minister were at an end; and, at the age of sixty-four, with the Liberals led by Gladstone enjoying a commanding majority in the House of Commons, it seemed that his career was over.

For a time it was as if Disraeli thought so too. He appeared less frequently in the Commons, pleading illness. Once again he was blamed for a Conservative defeat. Influential men in the party compared him unfavourably with his predecessor Lord Derby who, having died in October 1869, was no longer able to support him. Moves were made to have him replaced by Derby's son, now the fifteenth earl, who was naturally far more to the taste of the Conservative old guard. Disraeli's sinking reputation was not improved by the publication of *Lothair*, a novel, unlike its immediate predecessors, with no political purpose, which is now recognized as one of the best and most accomplished – certainly the most entertaining – of all Disraeli's books. It was an enormous popular success, both in England and America. But the critics did not like it; nor did his political colleagues who considered it a product unbecoming to the dignity of a former Prime Minister. 'His wisest friends think it must be a mistake,' wrote Monckton Milnes, 'and his enemies hope that it will be his ruin.'

Disraeli was little disturbed by this; but his wife's failing health was a constant worry to him. She had fallen seriously ill after a visit to Scotland in 1867 where – to celebrate the unexpected warmth of their welcome by a people whom Disraeli, in common with most statesmen of the time, offended by always talking about 'England', never 'Great Britain' – they had danced what they thought was a jig, 'or was it a hornpipe?', around their bedroom. On their return to London, Gladstone, who liked Mrs Disraeli, had referred sympathetically to her illness in a speech in the House. Disraeli responded with tears in his eyes to this graceful recognition that the two men's bitter animosity did not extend to their wives. Soon after, he himself fell ill; and, prevented by gout from visiting her sick-room across the corridor at Hughenden, took to writing her letters. She preserved them all carefully, wrapping them up in a packet labelled, 'Notes from dear Dizzy during our illness when we could not leave our rooms.'

She recovered sufficiently to attend a reception given at the Foreign Office – she deemed 10 Downing Street 'so dingy and decaying' – to celebrate his becoming Prime Minister. It was a grand affair, one of the season's great social events, with 'Dizzy in his glory', one of the guests recorded, 'leading about the Princess of Wales'. But his glory was overcast; in repose 'the impenetrable man' had looked 'low'; for his wife was obviously 'very ill and haggard'.

She was suffering from cancer of the stomach. To give some kind of reward to her before it was too late, Disraeli asked the Queen to create her a Viscountess on his resignation as Prime Minister, citing the precedents created by Baroness Chatham, wife of the elder Pitt, and Baroness Stratheden, wife of Sir John Campbell. The Queen did not like the suggestion which was 'very embarrassing'. But though she feared it would subject the strange woman to even more ridicule, she did not like to refuse Disraeli, to whom she gave her consent in a letter which bears no hint of her reluctance. Thereafter Mary Anne signed herself in letters to her beloved husband, 'your devoted Beaconsfield'.

Unaware that he already knew it, she tried to keep the nature of her disease a secret from her husband. Ill as she was, she insisted on accompanying him to dinners and parties, pretending to enjoy them for his sake, coming home exhausted, until she collapsed in the middle of an important reception and realized that she must go out no more. 'It tears my heart to see such a spirit suffer, and suffer so much,' Disraeli wrote. 'We have not been separated for thirty-three years and in all that time, in her society, I have never had a moment of dullness.'

To the end she refused to take to her bed, so long as she could sit up to be with him. And when she could not be with him she wrote him loving letters: 'My own dearest . . . I have nothing to tell you, except that I love you. . . . I miss you sadly. . . . I feel so grateful for your tender love and kindness. . . .' She died in her chair just before Christmas 1872 and was buried in the churchyard at Hughenden. For ten minutes Disraeli stood looking down upon the coffin in its grave, the cold wind blowing the rain against his black coat.

As an antidote for grief, he threw himself back into the political struggle. Already he had reasserted his authority in the Conservative party by some vigorous speeches both in the House of Commons and in the country at large, condemning the government's faltering, blundering record, comparing its Ministers to 'a range of exhausted volcanoes'. At Manchester he spoke for over three hours to a huge audience at the Free Trade Hall, attacking the government's weak foreign policy, its neglect of the Navy, presenting the Conservatives as the 'national party', protectors of 'the constitution of the country', of the Church, the Monarchy and the House of Lords, against those subversive radical forces which Gladstone declined to repudiate. At

The coat of arms of Viscountess Beaconsfield

Opposite: A moment of sadness and reflection, *c.* 1868

94

Disraeli visited Manchester in April 1872 and received a grand reception to a speech more than three hours in length, in which he defended Church, Lords and monarchy against radical attack. 'All classes vied in the cordiality of their welcome to the Conservative leader'

the Crystal Palace he repeated his assault on the Liberals, maintaining that the working classes, who had no patience with their 'continental' notions, and looked to the Conservatives for the improvement of their social conditions, were proud of 'belonging to a great country', 'to an Imperial country' whose power and sense of mission were 'to be attributed to the ancient institutions of the land'.

The great and new-found popularity which such brilliant speeches and warmly applauded opinions brought Disraeli was well demonstrated at the end of February 1872 during the celebrations to mark the recovery of the Prince of Wales from typhoid fever. On their way to the thanksgiving service in St Paul's, Gladstone's reception was cold, even hostile, Disraeli's warm and enthusiastic. On his return

Disraeli as a national figure, uniting the classes, the able representative of both landlord and tenant

from the Cathedral Disraeli was seen at the Carlton Club, staring into the distance while another member spoke to him, giving the impression that he was looking into another world. Sir William Fraser later asked Disraeli's companion what the conversation was about; and when told that it was merely some county business, Sir William observed, 'I will tell you what he was *thinking* about. He was thinking that he will be Prime Minister again.'

And so he was. Exercising great restraint and shrewdness, he refused to form a government in 1873 when Gladstone was defeated in his attempt to do what the Conservatives had failed to do, to establish a Roman Catholic University at Dublin. Disraeli sensed that, if he waited, the dissatisfactions and divisions in the Liberal party would become more pronounced; the people would become even more tired than they already were of what he called the Liberals' 'incessant and harassing legislation'; and the Conservatives, standing on a patriotic platform and promising gradual reform rather than continual upheaval, would win a clear victory. He was encouraged in this belief by the enormous improvement he had helped to bring about in the party's organization. Some years before he had entrusted John Eldon Gorst, a clever young barrister and former Fellow of St John's College, Cambridge, with the task of creating a Conservative Central Office in Whitehall and of ensuring that every constituency was contested by a candidate selected in advance. Gorst and Major Charles Keith-Falconer, as Secretary, also efficiently administered the reformed National Union of Conservative and Working Men's Associations, dropping the 'Working Men's' from the Associations' title at the

97

'"What a fight we might have for the crown, *now!*" the Unicorn said . . .'. When Alice encountered the lion and the unicorn in *Through the Looking-Glass*, Tenniel is believed to have depicted them as Gladstone and Disraeli in caricature. Lewis Carroll's own political sympathies lay very much with Disraeli

Above right: Prime Minister again: the 1874 election was a brilliant victory for the Conservatives, who won most of the county seats and made big gains in the larger boroughs

suggestion of Disraeli, who considered the words laid unnecessary emphasis on the class of their members.

Disraeli's faith in victory after this organization of the party's machinery was fully justified. In the general election of 1874 the Conservatives gained a majority of more than a hundred seats over the Liberals. Disraeli's triumph was complete when Lord Salisbury, formerly his most influential critic, was prevailed upon to join his Cabinet.

The Queen, of course, was as delighted as she had been when Disraeli had become Prime Minister before. 'You will see that instead of being a Govt. of Dukes as you might imagine,' she told her daughter in Germany, 'it will only contain 1 [the Duke of Richmond] and he a very sensible, honest, and highly respected one. The others are all distinguished and able men not at all retrograde.' Indeed, it was a highly promising government, drawn from all sections of the party, and well qualified to keep the Liberals in their now subordinate place.

Its task was much eased by the retirement of Gladstone who 'deeply desired', as he put it himself, 'an interval between Parliament and the grave'. And so, with the Opposition in disarray and with a large majority, Disraeli was able to carry with ease several major measures of social reform. These included two important Trade Union Acts, a consolidating Public Health Act, a Factory Act, an Act to safeguard the funds of Friendly Societies, an Agricultural Holdings Act, an Artisans' Dwelling Act, and the Sale of Food and Drugs Act. It was a programme of which the author of *Sybil* and a former leader of Young England could well be proud; and Disraeli was justified in taking a large share of the credit for a policy which he described as one round which 'the country [could] rally', even though he took little interest in its details.

He was not in fact much concerned with the details of government, only in the pursuit of general policies. At Cabinet meetings he talked little; and outside the Cabinet he left his Ministers to run their departments in their own way, reluctant to dismiss the failures, loyally taking the responsibility for their errors. Yet he was by no means a weak Prime Minister. There was never any doubt that he was in charge. Conciliatory and approachable, polite and even-tempered, he was nevertheless inflexible when his mind was made up, always ready to exercise his power in the realization of important aims. He kept Ministers on a loose rein, but they were always aware that the rein was there and that when necessary he would tighten it.

Over the Queen he could not exercise the same dominion. On occasions, indeed, he was obliged to demur to the wishes of the Faery – as he referred to her in allusion, less ironic than affectionate, to Spenser's

The visitors' sitting-room at Osborne. On his first meeting with Queen Victoria there after winning the 1874 election, Disraeli was invited to sit down; no Prime Minister since Melbourne had received *that* favour from the Queen

Disraeli was not anxious to
intervene when rebellion against the
Turks spread from Herzegovina to
Bosnia in the second half of 1875
(*right*), but he was determined that
British interests should be taken
account of when threatened by the
alliance of the three emperors of
Austria, Germany and Russia
(*below*)

Faerie Queene. He had to yield to her, for instance, over the Royal Titles Bill by which the Queen was enabled to assume the long-desired title of Empress of India at a politically inconvenient time. But his personal relationship with her grew closer and closer: she permitted him to sit down during audiences and to write to her in the first person letters couched in the most outlandishly romantic terms. And she allowed herself to be persuaded by cajoling flattery to do things no one else could have induced her to do. 'He has got the length of her foot exactly, and knows how to be sympathetic,' commented the Queen's Secretary, Henry Ponsonby. 'He seems to me always to speak in a burlesque . . . with his tongue in his cheek. But are not her woes told in the same manner? . . . He communicates . . . boundless professions of love and loyalty. He is most clever. . . . In fact, I think him cleverer than Gladstone with his terrible earnestness.'

The Queen worried about his health. And she had good cause to do so. For much of the time now he was ill, suffering from intermittent attacks of gout, from asthma and bronchitis. It was clear that the strain of the premiership was proving too much for a constitution which had never been robust. He expressed a wish to resign, but was persuaded instead to go to the House of Lords as Earl of Beaconsfield. On 11 August 1876 he made his last speech in the Commons. Before leaving he stood for a moment at the bar of the House, silently gazing up to the galleries and across the benches, the scenes of past failures and past triumphs.

It was only after Disraeli's last speech in the Commons, on 11 August 1876, that it was made known to the newspapers that he was henceforward to be Earl of Beaconsfield

While there were no more triumphs to come in the House of Commons, Disraeli's days of greatness were not yet over: he still had a part to play on a wider and grander stage. So far in his career he had had little chance of displaying his formidable gifts in what a character in one of his books describes as 'real politics: foreign affairs'. Indeed, he did not appear particularly suited to deal with foreign affairs: he could speak no foreign language except French, and that extremely badly. He had rarely been abroad since his youth, and had the vaguest grasp of geography. Although always ready to attack the Liberals for what he condemned as their responsibility for England's decline as a great power, neither in opposition nor in office did he seem to have any constructive ideas on foreign policy: on what was now the main issue of the day, the Eastern Question, his views were at variance with public opinion in the country as a whole. Having no sympathy with nationalist movements, he did not share the general feelings of outrage at reports of the cruel misrule of the Christian subjects of the still huge, though ramshackle Turkish Empire. He would have preferred, in fact, to let the Eastern Question alone, and was only anxious lest the Dreikaiserbund, the League of the Three Emperors (of Austria, Germany and Russia), would steal a march on him. If there were capital to make out of the Question, he was determined to make it himself.

As it happened, he stole a march on his rivals over a matter only indirectly concerned with the Turkish Empire, the Suez Canal. In October 1875 the Sultan's bankruptcy led to the ruin of the Khedive of Egypt, who was thereby forced to look for a purchaser of the shares he owned in the Suez Canal Company. As the French already owned the rest of the ordinary shares, the Khedive turned in the first instance to them, entering into negotiations with two competing French syndicates, neither of which in the end could raise the money. As soon as he heard of these negotiations, Disraeli made up his mind that the British, not the French, must have the Khedive's shares. The Cabinet did not agree with him. But he persuaded them that 'the thing *must* be done'; and Montagu Corry was dispatched post-haste to Baron Rothschild to borrow the money which could not be raised in Parliament as it was in recess. According to Corry, Rothschild asked only two questions, 'When?' and, after eating a grape and spitting out the skin, 'What is your security?' The next day £4,000,000 was lent to the British government at $2\frac{1}{2}$ per cent. The Rothschilds earned £100,000 and the British government acquired the Khedive's shares.

'It is just settled; you have it, Madam,' Disraeli wrote proudly to the Faery who was subsequently reported to be 'in ecstasies'. 'The French Government', he added inaccurately, making the most of the story, 'has been out-generalled.' The *coup* was not as significant as Disraeli

made it out to be: the purchased shares represented less than half the total and were, in any case, mortgaged until 1895. But it was certainly a profitable investment: before the century was out the shares were worth well over six times as much as at the time of their purchase and were increasing in value year by year. Disraeli's reputation for financial acumen, though resting on rather shaky foundations, was secure.

His reputation as a European statesman was soon to be greatly enhanced when further troubles in the Turkish Empire provided him with fresh opportunities to display his remarkable abilities to an international audience.

Disraeli's initial response to these troubles was far from irreproachable. When French and German Consuls at Salonika were murdered by Muslim rioters, he declined to associate the British government with a protest made to Turkey by the Dreikaiserbund. But this display of independence merely encouraged the Porte 'to refuse to listen to advice', as the Queen feared it would, and to look to Britain for support in its difficulties. A few weeks later the *Daily News* published a horrifying story of fearful atrocities committed by Turkish irregular troops on Bulgarian peasants, 25,000 of whom were believed to have been murdered. Predisposed to prefer the Turks to their subject peoples, and encouraged in his prejudice by the Turcophil British

Disraeli's success in purchasing the Suez Canal shares was not appreciated across the Channel. 'Putting everything into his pocket, shares as well as vendor'

By playing down the stories of Turkish atrocities on Bulgarian peasants – mere 'coffee-house babble' – Disraeli was able to pose as the champion of English interests against threats of Russian expansionism into Turkish territory

Ambassador at Constantinople, Disraeli made light of the reports; and even when it became clear that, while the *Daily News*'s accounts were exaggerated, terrible slaughter had indeed taken place, he continued to talk dismissively of 'coffee-house babble' and to refer to the 'atrocities' in inverted commas, as though they were figments of some journalist's imagination.

The country in general took a different view; and Gladstone, outraged by the reports and sensing the time had come to emerge from his premature retirement, gave voice to this dissent in his famous, fiercely condemnatory pamphlet, *The Bulgarian Horrors and the Question of the East*, which sold 200,000 copies within a month.

The scene was now set for one of the bitterest political arguments that has ever erupted in England. People ranged themselves on the side of the Turks or on that of the Russians, protectors of the Slavs and the Turks' traditional enemies, decrying those who stood behind the opposing barricades with the most ferocious animosity. To Disraeli, Gladstone's pamphlet, which denounced the Turkish race as 'the one great anti-human specimen of humanity', was contemptible, 'vindictive and ill-written', 'perhaps the greatest . . . of all the Bulgarian horrors', the product of an 'unprincipled maniac'. To the Queen, its author, 'that half madman', was a 'mischief maker and firebrand', his conduct 'shameful' and 'most reprehensible'. The supporters of Gladstone, whose hatred of Disraeli was now fixed and intense, were equally ferocious and even more insulting: Edward Freeman, the historian, wrote of Disraeli, that 'Jew in his drunken insolence'.

As the arguments raged and the insults flew, Disraeli became increasingly anti-Russian, going so far as to declare in a speech at the Lord Mayor's Banquet that England's military resources were inexhaustible, and that once she entered into a war she would not stop fighting till right was done. By the beginning of 1878, after the refusal of the Turks to agree to a programme of reforms proposed by the Conference of Constantinople had led to Russia's declaration of war on Turkey, it seemed, indeed, that the English army would soon be on the march, despite the efforts of the Foreign Secretary, Lord Derby, to prevent it by revealing Cabinet secrets to the Russian Ambassador. Certainly the English people were ready for war; and the London music-halls rang to the raucous sound of the chorus of a song which added a new word to the English language:

> *We don't want to fight, but, by jingo if we do,*
> *We've got the ships, we've got the men, we've got the money too.*

The Queen – who offered to make Disraeli a Knight of the Order of the Garter and who heard without surprise that Gladstone had been jeered in the street – sympathized with the people's emotion. Horrified by Lord Derby's conduct and terrified that the Russians might seize Constantinople, she wrote to Disraeli, 'Oh if the Queen were a man, she would like to go and give those horrid Russians whose word one cannot trust such a beating.'

Disraeli himself seems not to have wanted war but he evidently believed that England ought to threaten war in the hope that peace might be preserved without loss of honour. He had, therefore, to tread

Disraeli warned against Russian territorial ambitions; his provocation, said Gladstone, was 'almost incredible'

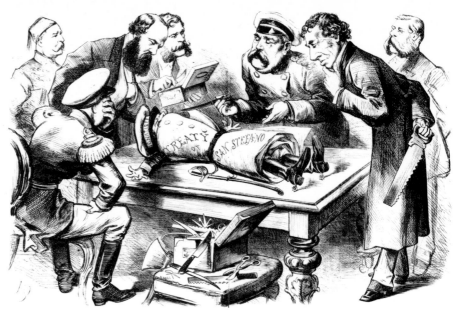

Disraeli resolved on strong resistance to Russia after the Treaty of San Stefano, which had been imposed on the Turks by General Ignatyev and had given a strong fillip to Russian interests

an extremely slippery path between those members of his own government who considered war against Russia on the side of the Turks utterly inconceivable and those who sympathized with the Queen's protest that she would 'lay down her crown . . . rather than submit to Russian insult'. At one moment he was condemned for being too bellicose, at another he was shouted at by a lady at a banquet who angrily demanded what was he 'waiting for' – to which question he replied with his customary suavity, 'At this moment for peas and potatoes, Madam.' In the end his delicately balanced policy was successful. Hearing of the formation of a British expeditionary force, and warned that war would be declared if the Russians threatened the Dardenelles, Prince Gorchakov, the Russian Chancellor, held back. Constantinople, too, was saved because, although the Tsar was in favour of seizing it, orders were never given to the army commander, his brother, the Grand Duke Nicholas, who, in any case, was so unnerved by the announcement that the British government had called up the reserves that he could not bring himself to take a step that might bring down ruin upon his small army.

Having successfully prevented the Russians from moving down to the Dardanelles and occupying Constantinople, Disraeli nevertheless continued with his far from secret preparations for war, since he was determined not to allow the Russians to get away with the terms, harsh to the victims and damaging to British interests, which had been imposed upon the Turks by the Treaty of San Stefano. Fortunately there were Russians, too, who recognized that the Treaty, if not amended, would inevitably lead to trouble for their country in the

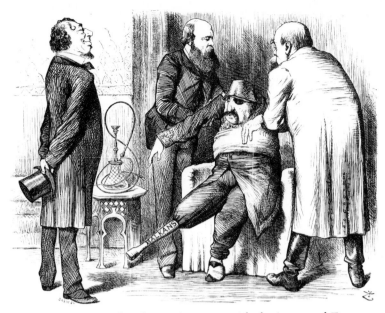

future. So they agreed to discuss its terms with the interested European powers, and to attend a congress in Berlin where a final settlement could be ratified.

Although he was now seventy-three and exhausted by the work and worry of the past few months, Disraeli made up his mind to attend the congress himself. To the profound relief of the Queen, who considered it an 'unmixed blessing', Derby had now resigned as Foreign Secretary; so Disraeli would be accompanied by Derby's able successor, Lord Salisbury, whose previous distrust of Disraeli had now turned to admiration and respect. In the knowledge that he could confidently leave all the tiresome details to Salisbury, who was in agreement with him as to the main lines of the policy to be pursued, Disraeli left for Berlin on 7 June 1878. This was six days before the congress was due to begin; but he wanted to allow himself plenty of time to rest on the way so that when he arrived he would not find the conferences and receptions too much of a strain.

His first meeting with Bismarck, the German Chancellor who presided as 'honest broker' over the congress, was not an unqualified success; but after a few days the two men found that they had so much in common – sharing the same realistic attitudes towards the problems of the day and the same indifference towards the inconvenient claims of troublesome but inconsiderable peoples such as the Balkan Slavs – that each was prepared to speak highly of the other. To Disraeli, Bismarck, though excessively loquacious, was 'a man of destiny'. Bismarck, in turn, remarked admiringly of Disraeli, 'Der alte Jude, das ist der Mann'.

Disraeli and Salisbury attend to the problems posed by Turkish weakness

The Congress of Berlin. Bismarck
visits Disraeli at the Kaiserhof
Hotel; Disraeli walks on the arm of
Montagu Corry. Never before had
an English Prime Minister left to act
as the country's representative at a
Continental conference while
Parliament was sitting. Bismarck
opened the Congress in English;
and no one could be exactly sure
whether this was done in a
patronizing or deferential spirit.
Disraeli also made his opening
address in English, not French,
much to the annoyance of the
Russians

Vor dem
Congress-Palais

Vor dem Kaiserhofe

Earl of Beaconsfield

Hoisting the British flag in Cyprus, formerly a part of the Turkish empire: a result of the 1878 negotiations

Few people in Berlin disagreed with him. Proud of Disraeli, her mother's friend, the Crown Princess arranged grand receptions for him at Potsdam. Elsewhere no dinner was deemed complete without him; no diplomat or minister could feel content who had not been privileged by a few minutes of his attentive conversation. His personality overshadowed the other delegations; and though his views did not always prevail, and other less conspicuous plenipotentiaries (such as the Austrian) gained more of their objectives, it was Disraeli whom those who attended the congress were afterwards most vividly to remember. Before the final document was signed he had to agree to Turkey's loss of more territory than he would have liked; but he returned to England having gained Cyprus for the Queen and having thus secured what he termed a *place d'armes* from which Russian designs on the crumbling Turkish Empire could be resisted.

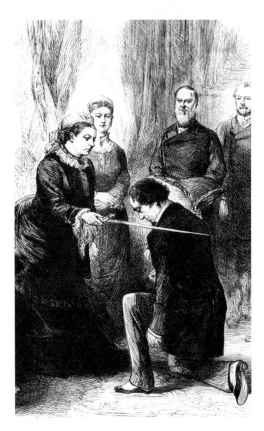

Salisbury and Disraeli were both
honoured with the Order of the
Garter after the Congress of Berlin

Disraeli arrived back in England to a hero's welcome. Large crowds
cheered him enthusiastically as he drove from the railway station to
Downing Street. 'High and low are delighted,' the Queen assured
him, 'excepting Mr Gladstone who is frantic.' She offered him a
dukedom, which he refused, and repeated her offer of the Garter,
which he accepted on condition that Lord Salisbury was also thus
honoured.

He was now at the height of his fame and popularity. He still had
his enemies. He was still abused by men like Carlyle who considered
him 'a cursed Jew, not worth his weight in cold bacon'. But the people
as a whole now admired and respected him deeply. Ever since the
death of his wife, and the fine and moving speeches which he made
while grieving over his loss, attitudes to Disraeli had been changing.
His unscrupulous past and cynical opportunism were being largely
forgotten or forgiven. He was gradually becoming recognized not only
as the prophet of a new Conservatism, at once compassionate at home
and positive abroad, but as a great statesman whom the Queen did
well to honour. Power had brought responsibility. By 1878 the
transformation in public attitudes towards Disraeli was complete.

The triumphant Disraeli in August
1878: toasted by the Carlton Club
(*left*) and presented, with Salisbury,
with the freedom of the City of
London (*below*)

With friends at Hughenden. From left to right: standing are Montagu Corry, the Earl of Bradford and Lord Wharncliffe; and sitting are Lady Bradford, Lady Wharncliffe and Disraeli himself. The Earl of Pembroke lies at front

As he walked down Whitehall leaning on Montagu Corry's arm, straightening his back with an effort when he felt himself being watched, the still black curls carefully arranged in the centre of his forehead, rings worn over the fingers of his white gloves, men respectfully raised their hats to him as he passed. Although his tired, rouged face and painful bronchitic breathlessness seemed to belie the fact, he delighted in the incessant round of dinner-parties, receptions, weddings and soirées to which he was invited. He had plenty of time for such pleasures, for his trusted and hard-working private secretaries saw to it that he was not bothered with the humdrum routine and detailed work which he detested, while the Foreign Office, the only department with whose affairs he had felt it necessary as a Prime Minister to be fully acquainted, could now be left in the capable hands of Salisbury. This left a large part of his days free for attending to the pleasurable business of dispensing honours and patronage and to the writing of letters.

Most of these letters were now addressed to Lady Bradford, the wife of the fourth Earl of Bradford and daughter of a Shropshire landowner

Lady Chesterfield. Disraeli enjoyed the company of her and her sister Lady Bradford. He lived, he said, only for 'the delightful society of the two persons I love most in the world'

who had helped Disraeli obtain the nomination for Shrewsbury as a young man. Five years before, at the age of sixty-eight, he had fallen in love with her. Had she been free he would no doubt have liked to marry her. Mary Anne had left him a letter to read after her death: 'My own dear husband . . . God bless you my dearest kindest. You have been a perfect husband to me. . . . Do not live alone dearest. Someone I earnestly hope you may find as attached to you as your own devoted Mary Anne.'

Lady Bradford was certainly not as attached to him as Mary Anne. Indeed, she seems to have become rather tired and exasperated by the effusive devotion of a man fourteen years older than herself who assured her that to see her, or at least to hear from her every day, was 'absolutely necessary' to his existence. His passion for her was so intense that he asked her widowed, elder sister, Lady Chesterfield, to marry him instead, mainly, if not entirely (it was supposed) so that he would be able to spend more time with the object of his true devotion. Presumably well aware of his motives, Lady Chesterfield declined the offer.

IN
MEMORY
OF
LT. & ADJT. TEIGNMOUTH MELVILL,
AND LT. NEVILL J. A. COGHILL,
1ST. BATTN. 24TH. REGIMENT WHO
DIED ON THIS SPOT 22ND JAN.
1879,
TO SAVE
THE
QUEEN'S
COLOR
OF THEIR
REGIMENT.

A British force of 1,200 was totally destroyed by a Zulu *impi* of 20,000 in January 1879. Disraeli could not avoid some of the criticisms that followed

She seems, however, to have taken no offence; and, from that time on, she, as well as her sister, continued to receive a stream of letters from Disraeli's busy pen. He had found time to write to them both from Berlin; and he found even more time once he was home again to record the details of his social life, to describe with an exaggerated dismay that did not disguise his real pleasure, the hazards of dining out, the fearful cold at Windsor, 'that castle of the winds' where it was a breach of etiquette to blow one's nose during an audience, the even more frightful cold, both of atmosphere and food, in another house where he was driven to exclaim, when champagne was served, 'Thank God for something warm!'

Although he still relished his social life, Disraeli could no longer summon the energy to give his government the firm leadership which might have enabled it to survive the worsening agricultural and economic depression at home and its successive troubles abroad. For the most serious of these troubles – an unnecessary war against the Afghans and another war in South Africa in which the Zulus destroyed a British force at Isandhlwana – the blame could be attached to disobedient and high-handed officials on the spot rather than to the Prime Minister at home. But Disraeli naturally had to face fierce criticism from his opponents for the mistakes of his government and its servants. And not all this criticism was unjustified: when the errors of Bartle Frere, the High Commissioner for South Africa, became known he was neither dismissed nor fully backed, but given a rebuke

accompanied by an assurance that confidence in him had not been withdrawn. This understandably prompted a leading Liberal to read out in the Commons an imaginary letter to the High Commissioner from the Colonial Secretary: 'Dear Sir Bartle Frere, I cannot think you are right. Indeed, I think you are very wrong; but after all you know a great deal better than I do. I hope you won't do what you are going to do; but if you do I hope it will turn out well.'

These mistakes, accompanied by an economic slump, gave Gladstone just the kind of ammunition which he needed to attack the 'wasteful' and 'disgraceful' imperial policies of his rival. In a series of famous speeches in Scotland, where he was standing for Midlothian, he spoke with a fervour that stirred his mass audiences of 'the sanctity of life in the hill villages of Afghanistan' being as 'inviolable in the eye of Almighty God as can be your own'. Disraeli dismissed Gladstone's 'drenching . . . wearisome rhetoric' on these 'pilgrimages of passion' as so much 'rhodomontade and rigmarole'. But he would make no effective reply to it; nor could his colleagues in the Cabinet, the most effective orators being disqualified as peers from public speaking during an election campaign. Nor yet was the Tory organization any match for the well-run machine of their opponents during the general election of 1880.

Disraeli awaited the results of the election at Hatfield, drinking Lord Salisbury's 'exquisite' wine and affecting confidence in victory. The resounding defeat when it came surprised even his most

Hatfield House. Salisbury's Grand Château Margaux, served there in an 1870 vintage, provided a pleasant preliminary for Disraeli before the shock of electoral defeat in the 1880 election

The drawing-room at Hughenden: Mary Anne's portrait over the fireplace, Queen Victoria's at left

pessimistic supporters. But he accepted it with calm equanimity; and while Gladstone wrote exultantly of 'the downfall of Beaconsfieldism' being like 'the vanishing of some vast magnificent castle in an Italian romance', Disraeli prepared to return to Hughenden. And there, having arranged for Montagu Corry to be granted a peerage and taken leave of the Queen, who contemplated with horror having now to deal with '*that half mad firebrand* who wd soon ruin everything & be a Dictator', he settled down to the contemplation of his trees, reading books over his solitary meals, and the writing of more books of his own.

He began by finishing a novel which he had begun several years before. This was *Endymion*, the story of the twins, Endymion and Myra, who survive the misfortune of their father's impoverishment and death to rise to eminence in the social world. It is a book full of well-drawn characters and of entertaining social and political comment. But its contents were not of primary concern to the publisher, Norton Longman, who was so confident of selling large numbers of any new novel by Disraeli that he offered the enormous sum of £10,000 without having read it. In September 1881 he went over to Hughenden to collect the manuscript.

He found Disraeli in 'capital spirits', with a whim to invest a simple transaction with an air of intrigue and mystery. His host, speaking in hushed tones, led him up to the study where he insisted on short-sightedly lighting the candles himself as he did not wish to excite the suspicions of the servants. Disraeli produced the three handwritten volumes, each 'carefully tied up in red tape', and laid them in a red despatch box. These boxes were then carried to Longman's room with such care and silence that the publisher felt as though he and the author were 'about to rob a church'.

'What are you going to do with them?' Disraeli whispered, having closed the door 'with extra precaution'.

'A happy thought flashed across my mind,' Longman recorded. '"My Glad———" I luckily stopped in time – "bag!"' So the boxes were secreted in his Gladstone bag, and the next morning were removed from the house.

Less than three months later the novel was published; and so nervous was Disraeli that it would not justify the huge amount which Longman had paid for it that he offered to cancel the agreement in exchange for a fixed royalty on each copy sold. But he need not have worried. The critics were kind; and, though the original edition did not sell as many copies as *Lothair*, a subsequent cheap edition enabled the publishers 'to make a profit out of the bargain'.

Encouraged by Longman's faith in *Endymion*, Disraeli immediately settled down to write another novel in which, in the character of Falconet, he intended to satirize Gladstone, that 'wicked man' of 'maniacal vanity' for whom he had recently conceived a far greater dislike than he had ever felt in the earlier years of their rivalry. He sat down to the book with evident relish and completed the first few chapters during the pleasant Indian summer of 1880.

The book was never finished. The mild autumn of 1880 was followed by a harsh winter of snowstorms and bitterly cold east winds. Disraeli attended the House of Lords in January to attack the government for its 'perpetual and complete reversal of all that has occurred'; but he did not feel strong enough to say all that he wanted to say and sat down exhausted.

Weakened by bronchitis and asthma, probably by Bright's disease and certainly by insomnia, his health had been further undermined by the deleterious medicines which his doctors had in the past prescribed. In 1877 he had been persuaded to consult a homoeopath, Joseph Kidd, who had had the bottles of the more harmful medicines thrown away, had recommended his patient to drink claret rather than port, and had advised him not to eat pastry or pudding at his evening meal. Gradually, under the care of Kidd, the 'best medical man' his patient had ever known, Disraeli's health was improved, though he steadfastly

Last appearance in Parliament, Montagu Corry behind him

refused to take any exercise. But the improvement was no more than a temporary respite. His bronchial trouble grew worse, exacerbated perhaps by Kidd's prescription of arsenic to clear the tubes; and he began also to suffer from uraemia which made him so drowsy when he went out to dinner that his neighbours sometimes thought he had fallen asleep. Once at Balmoral, the Queen's Secretary, Henry Ponsonby, observed how 'indolent and worn out' he seemed. 'He shot little arrows into the general discourse pungent and lively and then sat perfectly silent as if it were too much trouble to talk.' These shafts of wit grew more and more rare; and sometimes he would sit slumped in his chair throughout an entire meal, apparently heedless of the conversation being held around him, peering and poking at the food on his plate.

Returning home one night in March 1881 he caught a chill which soon developed into bronchitis. Two leading chest specialists were called, but they could do little for him; and Disraeli himself felt that he was dying. 'Whatever the doctors may tell you,' he said to his friend, Sir Philip Rose, 'I do not believe I shall get well.'

The Queen made anxious enquiries to which he replied with a pencil that shook in his hand; and when he was asked if he would like her to visit him, he replied, making his last sad joke, 'No, it is better not. She would only ask me to take a message to Albert.'

His coughing grew worse, and caused him fearful pain. Yet he lingered on day after day, restless, sleeping little until, after Easter, he sank into a coma. In a moment of consciousness he murmured, 'I had rather live but I am not afraid to die.' These were the last coherent words he spoke. Soon after four o'clock on the morning of 19 April he suddenly pushed himself up from his pillows and stretched himself out, as was his custom when rising to reply in debate. Corry listened intently, but no words came: he sank back and died.

The Queen could 'scarcely see' for her 'fast falling tears', she wrote to Corry. 'Never had I *so* kind and devoted a Minister and very few such devoted friends. . . . I have lost *so* many dear and valued friends but none whose loss will be more keenly felt. To England (or rather Gt. Britain) and to the *World* his loss is immense.'

Her people shared her grief. Walking past the drawn blinds of the Carlton Club, one of them thought that England would 'always regret the passing of the greatest statesman of his time', that there was no one left who could take his place.

Gladstone, who had prayed that God Almighty might be near the pillow of his former enemy as he lay dying, considered that a state funeral in Westminster Abbey would be most appropriate to the people's mood. But Disraeli's will gave instructions that he was to be buried at Hughenden next to the remains of his 'late dear wife'. And so he was.

His grave at Hughenden. The Queen said she understood his desire to be buried there rather than in Westminster Abbey. He had always 'hated display', she observed

The memorial tablet above his pew at Hughenden Church, 'placed by his grateful Sovereign and Friend, Victoria R.I.' and surrounded by a wreath of what the Queen called 'His favourite flower', the primrose

The Queen did not attend the funeral, for custom prevented her. But she sent two wreaths of primroses, his favourite flowers, from Windsor; and she later drove down to Hughenden where the vault was reopened so that she could place some china flowers on the coffin. Nor did Gladstone attend the funeral, making the public excuse that he was too busy, but revealing in a private comment that he considered the private ceremony a final, characteristic show of conceit, 'all display without reality or genuineness'. In the House of Commons, Gladstone made some amends for this uncharitable verdict by speaking of Disraeli's 'great qualities', his 'remarkable power of self-government', his 'parliamentary courage'. But it was in the House of Lords that the most generous and unreserved tributes were heard. Here Lord Salisbury said that he would never forget the 'patience, gentleness, the unswerving and unselfish loyalty' of the great man under whose leadership he had been proud to serve. 'More and more as his life went on,' Salisbury continued, 'as the heat and turmoil of controversy were left behind', and as 'the gratification of every possible ambition' made it clear that he had no inferior motive, the people of his country, who had come to love and revere him, recognized that one burning desire 'dominated his actions'. 'Zeal for the greatness of England was the passion of his life.'

It was a fitting epitaph. No one doubted the depth and honesty of Disraeli's patriotism. Unmoved as he was by nationalist movements in all other countries, he never wavered in his fervent support of English nationalism and of England's Empire, in his belief in the greatness of a country in which he seemed so alien a figure. Of Disraeli's other motives and beliefs it was, and is, difficult to be so sure. There will always be argument about him, about the extent to which he was guided by opportunism and ambition rather than by principle, about the true feelings which lay beneath those sardonic features, that inscrutable irony. 'He was an enigma to his contemporaries,' as Lord Blake has observed, 'and he remains one even today.'

Sir Robert Ensor also wrote of the enigmatic nature of Disraeli: 'His party came to trust him, to idolize, and even to love; but they never understood him. And he, with his passion for England, remained deeply un-English. Idealist and cynic, prophet and tactician, genius and charlatan in one, men took him for a flaunting melodramatist until they experienced him as a deadly fighter. A radical by origin and instinct, he remade the conservative party; but though he ruled its counsels so long, it was only warily and within limits that he ever shaped them to his ideas. Disputes over his career have turned less on facts than on moral values. More than half a century after his death there is still argument about them.'

There is surely little doubt, though, that until 1846 when he helped to engineer the resignation of Peel, Disraeli was driven by an ambition to make his mark rather than by any consistent political purpose, and that his attacks on Peel would not have been so mounted had he been given in 1841 the office for which he had asked.

Very slowly after 1846, however, a rational and realistic policy can be discerned through the fog which he chose to cast over it with his romantic Tory philosophy and his fanciful interpretations of history. He believed that, although the greatness of England depended upon the ascendancy of the landed classes, the Conservative party must associate itself more closely with the business and commercial interests of the middle class, that, in fact, while Peel himself had been destroyed, Peel's policies must not die with him but be restored and refreshed. That he, a Jew with a far from respectable past, heavy debts and a dubious reputation, became and remained the leader of the Conservative party in the Commons at such a time was itself proof of his courage and parliamentary genius. His contemporary, the Duke of Argyll, dismissed the idea that there were any formidable obstacles in the way of his becoming leader. 'It is really nonsense', the Duke wrote, 'to talk of a man in such a position as a mere "Jew Boy" who by force of nothing but extraordinary genius attained to the leadership of a great party. The only impediments in his way were not in any want of external advantages but his own grotesque and unintelligible opinions.'

Yet, if Disraeli's origins were by no means obscure and his family never poor, he was undoubtedly an outsider in the hierarchy of his party. Not only his race and tastes and manner but even his education separated him from his colleagues: apart from the Irish Lords Naas and Cairns, he was the only member of both his first and second Cabinets who had not attended a famous public school; most had been to Eton. There is no doubt, too, that in the earlier years of his influence he constantly had to struggle against both a degree of dislike and prejudice which would have overborne a less determined, brave and resilient man, and a fierce resentment occasioned by the fact that the Conservatives could not manage without his great talents – as many of them would have liked to have done – since he was the only man who possessed them in such multiplicity, on his side of the House.

It was his triumphant achievement to use these abilities not only ultimately to provide his party with an efficient organization but also with a policy of social reform combined with imperialism which appealed to the country's new electorate and brought forward the Conservatives as an acceptable and practical alternative to the Liberals.

His bitter rivalry with Gladstone after the death of Palmerston was an important factor in this. In sharp contrast to the stern and moralistic Gladstone – anathematized by his enemy as that 'sophistical rhetorician, inebriated with the exuberance of his own verbosity' – whose radical reforms caused widespread alarm, Disraeli was able to present himself as a wise and worldly man of moderation and common sense, a believer in measures to alleviate the plight of the poorer classes, but above all as the leader of a national party with a concern for the interests of every class and a determination to ensure that the ideals of the Empire were sustained and the greatness of England in the world enhanced. As he said in a speech at the Guildhall in the year that he brought back what he described as 'peace with honour' from Berlin, 'One of the greatest of Romans, when asked what were his politics, replied, *Imperium et Libertas*. That would not make a bad programme for a British Ministry.'

1804	21 December: Disraeli born in London	1837	*Henrietta Temple* and *Venetia* published. July: returned as Conservative Member for Maidstone. December: makes disastrous maiden speech	1859	Government defeated. Palmerston becomes Prime Minister
1817	31 July: received into Church of England			1860–65	leader of Opposition once more
1818	attends Higham Hall school	1839	marries Mrs Wyndham Lewis	1866	Derby forms third minority government with Disraeli again Chancellor of the Exchequer
1821	articled to a firm of solicitors in the City	1841	at general election returned as Conservative Member for Shrewsbury, but Peel declines to give him office	1867	Reform Bill establishes him as hero of the Conservative party
1824	while on holiday in Germany decides not to be a lawyer. Autumn: engages in reckless speculation in South American mining shares	1843	established as most influential member of Young England	1868	becomes Prime Minister on Derby's retirement. Autumn: Conservatives defeated in general election. Disraeli resigns. Gladstone becomes Prime Minister
		1844	*Coningsby* published		
1825	the *Representative*, a newspaper which he has persuaded John Murray to back, is launched	1845	*Sybil* published	1870	*Lothair* published
		1846	attacks Peel over proposed repeal of Corn Laws and is recognized as one of the most able men in the Conservative party	1872	exercises firm control over Conservative party and defines its policy. December: death of his wife
1826	*Vivian Grey* published				
1830	sets out on a tour of the Mediterranean and the Middle East which lasts for sixteen months	1847	elected as Member for county of Buckinghamshire. *Tancred* published	1874	Gladstone defeated at the polls. Disraeli forms second administration
1832	*Contarini Fleming* published. June: stands unsuccessfully as Radical in by-election at High Wycombe	1848	purchases Hughenden Manor	1875	arranges purchase of the Khedive of Egypt's shares in the Suez Canal
		1852	becomes Chancellor of the Exchequer in Lord Derby's Cabinet. December: his budget brings the government down	1876	makes last speech in the House of Commons. Created Earl of Beaconsfield
1835	after his third defeat as a Radical at High Wycombe, he throws in his lot with the Conservatives and is invited to become the Tory candidate at Taunton where he is again defeated. December: *A Vindication of the English Constitution* published	1852–58	leads Opposition in House of Commons	1878	attends Congress of Berlin
		1858	becomes Chancellor of Exchequer again in Lord Derby's second Cabinet	1880	*Endymion* published
				1881	19 April: dies in London

LIST OF ILLUSTRATIONS

Osborne; *Illustrated London News*, August 1878

Pas de Deux; cartoon by John Tenniel; *Punch*, August 1878

111 Carlton Club banquet at riding-school, Knightsbridge; *Illustrated London News*, August 1878

Presentation of Freedom of City of London to Lords Beaconsfield and Salisbury; *Illustrated London News*, 10 August 1878

112 Group at Hughenden; photograph by H.W. Taunt, 1874 (back row:

Montagu Corry, Earl of Bradford, Lord Wharncliffe; seated: Lady Bradford, Lady Wharncliffe, Disraeli; lying down: Earl of Pembroke)

113 Lady Chesterfield; photograph by H. Lenthal, 1871. Royal Archives, Windsor. By Gracious Permission of Her Majesty The Queen

114 Monument erected by Sir Bartle Frere at Isandhlwana, South Africa, in 1879; contemporary photograph. Royal Archives, Windsor. By Gracious Permission of Her Majesty The Queen

115 Hatfield House, south entrance. Photo

National Monuments Record, London

116 The drawing-room, Hughenden Manor; contemporary photograph. High Wycombe Library

118 Montagu Corry (1st Lord Rowton) and Lord Beaconsfield; engraving after sketch by Harry Furniss (1854–1925)

119 Lord Beaconsfield's grave; photo by H.W. Taunt. Oxford Central Library

120 Monument to Lord Beaconsfield, St Michael and All Angels, Hughenden; photo by H.W. Taunt, 1885. Oxford Central Library

BIBLIOGRAPHICAL NOTE

The official biography is *The Life of Benjamin Disraeli, Earl of Beaconsfield* by William Flavelle Monypenny and George Earle Buckle (revised edition, 2 vols., 1929). The best modern biography – indeed, one of the finest political biographies of recent times – is Robert Blake's *Disraeli* (1966). A good shorter work is *Disraeli* by R.W. Davis (1976). *Benjamin Disraeli* by Richard A. Levine (1968) provides an interesting study of the novels. *The Young Disraeli* (1960) by B.R. Jerman gives a comprehensive account of the early years. An entertaining popular biography is *Dizzy* (1951) by Hesketh Pearson.

Other recommended biographies
BEELEY, Harold, *Disraeli* (1936)
BLAKE, Robert, *Disraeli and Gladstone* (1970)
FRASER, Sir William, *Disraeli and His Party* (1891)
FROUDE, J.A., *Lord Beaconsfield* (1890)
KEBBEL, T.E., *Lord Beaconsfield* (1888)
MAUROIS, André, *Disraeli: A Picture of the Victorian Age* (new edition, 1962)
MEYNELL, Wilfrid, *The Man Disraeli* (revised edition, 1927)
ROTH, Cecil, *The Earl of Beaconsfield* (1952)
SICHEL, Walter, *Disraeli: A Study in Personality and Ideas* (1904)
SOMERVELL, D.C., *Disraeli and Gladstone* (1938)

Disraeli's works, speeches and letters
DISRAELI, Ralph (ed.), *Home Letters, 1830–1831* (1885)

Lord Beaconsfield's Correspondence with his Sister, 1832–1852 (1886)
KEBBEL, T.E. (ed.), *Selected Speeches of the Earl of Beaconsfield* (2 vols., 1882)
LONDONDERRY, Marchioness of (ed.), *The Letters of Benjamin Disraeli to Frances Anne, Marchioness of Londonderry* (1938)
Novels and Tales by the Earl of Beaconsfield (Hughenden edition, 11 vols., 1881)
SWARTZ, M. and H. (eds.), *Disraeli's Reminiscences* (1975)
ZETLAND, Marquess of (ed.), *The Letters of Disraeli to Lady Bradford and Lady Chesterfield* (2 vols., 1929)

Biographies of contemporaries
CECIL, Lady Gwendolen, *The Life of Robert, Marquis of Salisbury* (Vols. 1 and 2, 1921)
DISRAELI, Benjamin, *Lord George Bentinck: A Political Biography* (1852)
FEUCHTWANGER, E.J., *Gladstone* (1976)
GASH, Norman, *Sir Robert Peel* (1972)
JONES, W.D., *Lord Derby and Victorian Conservatism* (1956)
LONGFORD, Elizabeth, *Victoria RI* (1964)
LYTTON, Earl of, *The Life of Edward Bulwer, First Lord Lytton* (2 vols., 1913)
MAGNUS, Sir Philip, *Gladstone: A Biography* (1954)
MORLEY, John, *Life of William Ewart Gladstone* (3 vols., 1903)
PONSONBY, Arthur, *Henry Ponsonby: His Life from his Letters* (1942)
RHODES JAMES, Robert, *Rosebery* (1963)
TREVELYAN, G.M., *The Life of John Bright* (1913)

WHIBLEY, Charles, *Lord John Manners and His Friends* (2 vols., 1925)

The background
ADELMAN, Paul *Disraeli, Gladstone and Later Victorian Politics* (1972)
ARGYLL, Duke of, *Autobiography and Memoirs* (2 vols., 1906)
BENSON, A.C. and ESHER, Viscount (eds.), *The Letters of Queen Victoria, 1837–1861* (3 vols., 1907)
BUCKLE, G.E. (ed.), *The Letters of Queen Victoria, Second Series, 1862–1886* (3 vols., 1926)
ENSOR, R.C.K., *England, 1870–1914* (new edition, 1964)
FEUCHTWANGER, E.J., *Disraeli, Democracy and the Tory Party* (1968)
GASH, Norman, *Politics in the Age of Peel* (1953)
GRINTER, Robin, *Disraeli and Conservatism* (1968)
HANHAM, H.J., *Elections and Party Management: Politics in the Time of Disraeli and Gladstone* (1959)
KITSON CLARK, G., *The Making of Victorian England* (1962)
SETON-WATSON, R.W., *Disraeli, Gladstone and the Eastern Question* (1935)
SMITH, Paul, *Disraelian Conservatism and Social Reform* (1967)
SOUTHGATE, Donald, *The Passing of the Whigs, 1832–1886* (1962)
WOODWARD, Sir Llewellyn, *The Age of Reform, 1815–1870* (new edition 1964)
VINCENT, J.R. (ed.), *Disraeli, the Conservative Party and the House of Derby* (1977)